Penguin Education
Voices The third book

Voices The third book

Also available

Voices The first book   **Voices** The second book
Voices Teachers' handbook

edited by Geoffrey Summerfield

With over 30 pages of illustrations

Penguin Books

For C.M.L. Con Amore

Penguin Books Ltd, Harmondsworth,
Middlesex, England
Penguin Books Australia Ltd, Ringwood,
Victoria, Australia

First published 1968
Reprinted 1968 (twice), 1969, 1970 (twice), 1971
This selection copyright © Geoffrey Summerfield, 1968

Made and printed in Great Britain by
Butler & Tanner Ltd, Frome and London
Set in Lumitype Baskerville

Contents

Voices   *7*

Tunes for Some Poems   *177*

Acknowledgements   *180*

List of Illustrations   *182*

Index of Titles   *183*

Index of First Lines   *185*

Index of Poets, Translators and Collectors   *189*

1 O Taste and See

The world is
not with us enough.
O taste and see

the subway Bible poster said,
meaning **The Lord,** meaning
if anything all that lives
to the imagination's tongue,

grief, mercy, language,
tangerine, weather, to
breathe them, bite,
savour, chew, swallow, transform

into our flesh our
deaths, crossing the street, plum, quince,
living in the orchard and being

hungry, and plucking
the fruit.

DENISE LEVERTOV

2 Well Water

What a girl called 'the dailiness of life'
(Adding an errand to your errand. Saying,
'Since you're up . . .' Making you a means to
A means to a means to) is well water
Pumped from an old well at the bottom of the world.
The pump you pump the water from is rusty
And hard to move and absurd, a squirrel-wheel
A sick squirrel turns slowly, through the sunny
Inexorable hours. And yet sometimes
The wheel turns of its own weight, the rusty
Pump pumps over your sweating face the clear
Water, cold, so cold! you cup your hands
And gulp from them the dailiness of life.

RANDALL JARRELL

3 Days

What are days for?
Days are where we live.
They come, they wake us
Time and time over.
They are to be happy in:
Where can we live but days?

Ah, solving that question
Brings the priest and the doctor
In their long coats
Running over the fields.

PHILIP LARKIN

4 Black Rook in Rainy Weather

On the stiff twig up there
Hunches a wet black rook
Arranging and rearranging its feathers in the rain.
I do not expect miracle
Or an accident

To set the sight on fire
In my eye, nor seek
Any more in the desultory weather some design,
But let spotted leaves fall as they fall,
Without ceremony, or portent.

Although, I admit, I desire,
Occasionally, some backtalk
From the mute sky, I can't honestly complain:
A certain minor light may still
Leap incandescent

Out of kitchen table or chair
As if a celestial burning took
Possession of the most obtuse objects now and then –
Thus hallowing an interval
Otherwise inconsequent

By bestowing largesse, honour,
One might say love. At any rate, I now walk
Wary (for it could happen
Even in this dull, ruinous landscape); sceptical,
Yet politic; ignorant

Of whatever angel may choose to flare
Suddenly at my elbow. I only know that a rook
Ordering its black feathers can so shine
As to seize my senses, haul
My eyelids up, and grant

A brief respite from fear
Of total neutrality. With luck,
Trekking stubborn through this season
Of fatigue, I shall
Patch together a content

Of sorts. Miracles occur,
If you care to call those spasmodic
Tricks of radiance miracles. The wait's begun again,
The long wait for the angel,
For that rare, random descent.

SYLVIA PLATH

5 The Swan

Bottomed by tugging combs of water
The slow and loath swan slews and looks
Coldly down through chutes of stilled chatter
Upon the shadows in flight among the stones.

Into abashed confusions of ooze
It dips, and from the muddy fume
The silver and flute-like fishes rise
Endlessly up through all their octaves of gloom,

To where the roofed swan suavely swings
Without qualm on the quivering wave
That laves it on, with elbowing wings held wide
Under its eyes' hugged look and architrave.

Jonquil-long its neck adjudicates
Its body's course; aloof and cool
It cons the nonchalant and unseeing air
With its incurious and dispassionate stare.

Slow, slow, it slides, as if not to chafe
The even sleeve of its approach
Stretched stiff and oval in front of it,
Siphoning it on, selfless, silent, and safe.

On that grey lake, frilled round with scufflings
Of foam and milled with muttering,
I saw lingering, late and lightless,
A single swan, swinging, sleek as a sequin.

Negligently bright, wide wings pinned back,
It mooned on the moving water,
And not all the close and gartering dark
Or gathering wind could lift or flatter

That small and dimming image into flight;
Far from shore and free from foresight,
Coiled in its own indifferent mood
It held the heavens, shores, waters and all their brood.

W. R. RODGERS

6 Snow Drop

The blanched melted snows
Fill the plant's stem, a capillary
Of heightened moisture. Air weights
Round a white head hanging
Above granuled earth.
There, are three scarab-like petals,
Open, an insect's carapace
With a creature in these, poised.
It does not move. A white
Cylinder with two
Thin bands of green, broken
Away where that part finishes.

There is no more.
The sun's heat reaches the flower
Of the snowdrop.

JON SILKIN

7 Frogs

Frogs sit more solid
Than anything sits. In mid-leap they are
Parachutists falling
In a free fall. They die on roads
With arms across their chests and
Heads high.

I love frogs that sit
Like Buddha, that fall without
Parachutes, that die
Like Italian tenors.

Above all, I love them because,
Pursued in water, they never
Panic so much that they fail
To make stylish triangles
With their ballet dancer's
Legs.

NORMAN MacCAIG

8 Four Orders

I am a trembling leaf
I am a withered arm
I am a sunken reef
I am a trampled worm.

Leaf, be the caterpillar's joy
Arm, enfold the new-born boy
Reef, flower into a coral isle
Worm, fertilize the soil.

RONALD BOTTRALL

9 The Loving Dexterity

The flower
    fallen
she saw it

    where
it lay
    a pink petal

intact
    deftly
placed it

    on
its stem
    again

WILLIAM CARLOS WILLIAMS

10 The Mother's Song

It is so still in the house.
There is a calm in the house;
The snowstorm wails out there,
And the dogs are rolled up with snouts under the tail.
My little boy is sleeping on the ledge,
On his back he lies, breathing through his open mouth.
His little stomach is bulging round –
Is it strange if I start to cry with joy?

ANONYMOUS Translated from the Eskimo by Peter Freuchen

11 Fragment XXXVII

Green thoughts are
Ice block on a barrow
Gleaming in July.
A little boy with bare feet
And jewels at his nose stands by.

ISAAC ROSENBERG

12 To an Old Lady

Ripeness is all; her in her cooling planet
Revere; do not presume to think her wasted.
Project her no projectile, plan nor man it;
Gods cool in turn, by the sun long outlasted.

Our earth alone given no name of god
Gives, too, no hold for such a leap to aid her;
Landing, you break some palace and seem odd;
Bees sting their need, the keeper's queen invader.

No, to your telescope; spy out the land;
Watch while her ritual is still to see,
Still stand her temples emptying in the sand
Whose waves o'erthrew their crumbled tracery;

Still stand uncalled-on her soul's appanage;
Much social detail whose successor fades,
Wit used to run a house and to play Bridge,
And tragic fervour, to dismiss her maids.

Years her precession do not throw from gear.
She reads a compass certain of her pole;
Confident, finds no confines on her sphere,
Whose failing crops are in her sole control.

Stars how much further from me fill my night.
Strange that she too should be inaccessible,
Who shares my sun. He curtains her from sight,
And but in darkness is she visible.

WILLIAM EMPSON

13 Follower

My father worked with a horse-plough,
His shoulders globed like a full sail strung
Between the shafts and the furrow.
The horses strained at his clicking tongue.

An expert. He would set the wing
And fit the bright steel-pointed sock.
The sod rolled over without breaking.
At the headrig, with a single pluck ·

Of reins, the sweating team turned round
And back into the land. His eye
Narrowed and angled at the ground,
Mapping the furrow exactly.

I stumbled in his hob-nailed wake,
Fell sometimes on the polished sod;
Sometimes he rode me on his back
Dipping and rising to his plod.

I wanted to grow up and plough,
To close one eye, stiffen my arm.
All I ever did was follow
In his broad shadow round the farm.

I was a nuisance, tripping, falling,
Yapping always. But today
It is my father who keeps stumbling
Behind me, and will not go away.

SEAMUS HEANEY

14 The Chinaman and the Florentine

This man for forty years studied a leaf;
This man the scattered leaves of the Universe.

This man lies in the earth at Ch'ang-hsi;
This, in a crypt at the crossroads in Ravenna.

HYAM PLUTZIK

15 Hay for the Horses

He had driven half the night
From far down San Joaquin
Through Mariposa, up the
Dangerous mountain roads,
And pulled in at eight a.m.
With his big truckload of hay behind the barn.
With winch and ropes and hooks
We stacked the bales up clean
To splintery redwood rafters
High in the dark, flecks of alfalfa
Whirling through shingle-cracks of light,
Itch of haydust in the sweaty shirt and shoes.
At lunchtime under Black oak
Out in the hot corral,
– The old mare nosing lunchpails,
Grasshoppers crackling in the weeds –
'I'm sixty-eight,' he said,
'I first bucked hay when I was seventeen.
I thought, that day I started,
I sure would hate to do this all my life.
And dammit, that's just what
I've gone and done.'

GARY SNYDER

16 Ute Mountain

'When I am gone,'
the old chief said,
'if you need me, call me,'
and down he lay, became stone.

They were giants then
(as you may see),
and we
are not the shadows of such men.

The long splayed Indian hair
spread ravelling out
behind the rocky head
in groins, ravines;

petered across the desert plain
through Colorado,
transmitting force
in a single undulant unbroken line

from toe to hair-tip: there
profiled, inclined away from one
are features, foreshortened, and the high
blade of the cheekbone.

Reading it so, the eye
can take the entire great
straddle of mountain-mass,
passing down elbows, knees, and feet.

'If you need me, call me.'
His singularity dominates the plain
as we call to our aid his image:
thus men make a mountain.

CHARLES TOMLINSON

17 After Looking into a Book Belonging to my Great-Grandfather Eli Eliakim Plutzik

I am troubled by the blank fields, the speechless graves.
Since the names were carved upon wood, there is no word
For the thousand years that shaped this scribbling fist
And the eyes staring at strange places and times
Beyond the veldt dragging to Poland.
Lovers of words make simple peace with death,
At last demanding, to close the door to the cold,
Only *Here lies someone*.
Here lie no one and no one, your fathers and mothers.

HYAM PLUTZIK

18 Extracts from 'The People, Yes'

'Isn't that an iceberg on the horizon, Captain?'
'Yes, Madam.'
'What if we get in a collision with it?'
'The iceberg, Madam, will move right along
    as though nothing had happened.'

. . . . . .

A Scotsman keeps the Sabbath and anything else he can lay his
    hands on, say the English.
A fighting Frenchman runs away from even a she-goat, say the
    Germans.
A Russian, say the Poles, can be cheated only by a gypsy, a
    gypsy by a Jew, a Jew by a Greek, and a Greek by the devil.
'If I owned Texas and hell I would rent Texas and move to
    hell,' said a famous general.
'That's right,' wrote a Texas editor. 'Every man for his own
    country.'
The Peloponnesians pulled these long ago, so did the Russians,
    the Chinese, even the Fijis with rings in their noses.
    Likewise:
An American is an Anglo-Saxon when an Englishman wants
    something from him: or:
When a Frenchman has drunk too much he wants to dance, a
    German to sing, a Spaniard to gamble, an Italian to brag, an
    Irishman to fight, an American to make a speech: or:
'What is dumber than a dumb Irishman?' 'A smart Swede.'
These are in all tongues and regions of men. Often they bring
    laughter and sometimes blood.
The propagandas of hate and war always monkey with the
    buzz-saw of race and nationality, breed and kin, seldom
    saying, 'When in doubt hold your tongue.'
In breathing spells of bloody combat between Christian nations
    the order goes out: 'Don't let the men in the front-line
    trenches fraternize!'

. . . . . .

aw nuts aw go peddle yer papers
where did ja cop dat monkeyface
    jeez ja see dat skirt
    did ja glom dat moll
who was tellin you we wuz brudders
how come ya get on dis side deh street
go home and tell yer mudder she wants yuh
chase yer shadder aroun deh corner
yuh come to me wid a lot uh arkymalarky
    a bing in de bean fer you yeah
how come ya get on dis side deh street
go home and get yer umbreller washed
    den get yer face lifted
dis corner is mine – see – dis corner is mine
gwan ja tink ya gonna get dis f'm me fer nuttin
    nobody gets nuttin fer nuttin
    gwan monkeyface peddle yer papers
ya can't kiss yerself in here   dis is all fixed

     . . . . . .

'How do you do, my farmer friend?'
'Howdy.'

'Nice looking country you have here.'
'Fer them that likes it.'
'Live here all your life?'
'Not yit.'

. . . . . .

'Yesterday,' said the college boy home on vacation, 'we autoed
    to the country club, golfed till dark, bridged a while, and
    autoed home.'
'Yesterday,' said the father, 'I muled to the cornfield and
    gee-hawed till sundown, then I suppered till dark, piped till
    nine, bedsteaded till five, breakfasted and went muling
    again.'

. . . . . .

Lawyer: What was the distance between the two towns?
Witness: Two miles as the cry flows.
Lawyer: You mean as the crow flies.
Judge: No, he means as the fly crows.

CARL SANDBURG

19 Georgian Marketplaces

Down with all Raphaels
and up with Flemish Rubens,
his fountains of fishtails,
his color and crudeness !

Here weekdays are feastdays
with oxcarts and gourds,
and women like tambourines
in bracelets and beads,

indigo of turkeys' wattles,
persimmon fruits   yellow *hurmas*, wine in bottles.
You're out of money ?
Have a drink on me !

Bless all the old girls
who trade here in lettuce –
only baobab trees
boast a similar girth !

Marketplaces, blazes
of fire and youthfulness !
Your flaming bronzes
of hands are alight

with the gleam of butter
and the gold of wine.
Three cheers for the painter
who brings you alive !

ANDREI VOZNESENSKY Translated from the Russian by Max Hayward

20 As Others See Us

With 'No Admittance' printed on my heart,
    I go abroad, and play my public part ;
And win applause – I have no cause to be
    Ashamed of that strange self that others see.

But how can I reveal to you, and you,
  My real self's hidden and unlovely hue?
How can I undeceive, how end despair
  Of this intolerable make-believe?

You must see with God's eyes, or I must wear
  My furtive failures stark upon my sleeve.

BASIL DOWLING

21   I Am

I am – yet what I am, none cares or knows;
  My friends forsake me like a memory lost:
I am the self-consumer of my woes –
  They rise and vanish in oblivions host,
Like shadows in love frenzied stifled throes
  And yet I am, and live – like vapours tost

Into the nothingness of scorn and noise,
  Into the living sea of waking dreams,
Where there is neither sense of life or joys,
  But the vast shipwreck of my lifes esteems;
Even the dearest that I love the best
  Are strange – nay, rather, stranger than the rest.

I long for scenes where man hath never trod
  A place where woman never smiled or wept
There to abide with my Creator God,
  And sleep as I in childhood sweetly slept,
Untroubling and untroubled where I lie
  The grass below, above, the vaulted sky.

JOHN CLARE

22   Africa's Plea

I am not you –
but you will not
give me a chance,
will not let me be *me*.

'If I were you' –
but you know
I am not you,
yet you will not
let me be *me*.

You meddle, interfere
in my affairs
as if they were yours
and you were me.

You are unfair, unwise,
foolish to think
that I can be you,
talk, act
and think like you.

God made me *me*.
He made you *you*.
For God's sake
Let me be *me*.

ROLAND TOMBEKAI DEMPSTER

23 As Kingfishers Catch Fire

As kingfishers catch fire, dragonflies dráw fláme;
As tumbled over rim in roundy wells
 Stones ring; like each tucked string tells, each hung bell's
Bow swung finds tongue to fling out broad its name;
Each mortal thing does one thing and the same:
Deals out that being indoors each one dwells;
Selves – goes itself; *myself* it speaks and spells,
Crying *Whát I dó is me: for that I came.*

Í say móre: the just man justices;
Keéps gráce: thát keeps all his goings graces;
Acts in God's eye what in God's eye he is –
Chríst – for Christ plays in ten thousand places,
Lovely in limbs, and lovely in eyes not his
To the Father through the features of men's faces.

GERARD MANLEY HOPKINS

Margin glosses:
plucked | sounds out
expresses itself
behaves justly

24 Telephone Conversation

The price seemed reasonable, location
Indifferent. The landlady swore she lived
Off premises. Nothing remained
But self-confession. 'Madam,' I warned,
'I hate a wasted journey – I am African.'
Silence. Silenced transmission of
Pressurized good-breeding. Voice, when it came,
Lipstick coated, long gold-rolled
Cigarette-holder pipped. Caught I was, foully.
'HOW DARK?' . . . I had not misheard . . . 'ARE YOU LIGHT
OR VERY DARK?' Button B. Button A. Stench
Of rancid breath of public hide-and-speak.
Red booth. Red pillar-box. Red double-tiered
Omnibus squelching tar. It *was* real! Shamed
By ill-mannered silence, surrender
Pushed dumbfoundment to beg simplification.
Considerate she was, varying the emphasis –
'ARE YOU DARK? OR VERY LIGHT?' Revelation came.
'You mean – like plain or milk chocolate?'
Her assent was clinical, crushing in its light
Impersonality. Rapidly, wave-length adjusted,
I chose. 'West African sepia' – and as afterthought,
'Down in my passport.' Silence for spectroscopic
Flight of fancy, till truthfulness clanged her accent
Hard on the mouthpiece. 'WHAT'S THAT?' conceding
'DON'T KNOW WHAT THAT IS.' 'Like brunette.'
'THAT'S DARK, ISN'T IT?' 'Not altogether.
Facially, I am brunette, but, madam, you should see
The rest of me. Palm of my hand, soles of my feet
Are a peroxide blond. Friction, caused –
Foolishly, madam – by sitting down, has turned
My bottom raven black – One moment, madam!' – sensing
Her receiver rearing on the thunderclap
About my ears – 'Madam,' I pleaded, 'wouldn't you rather
See for yourself?'

WOLE SOYINKA

25 Summer Farm

Straws like tame lightnings lie about the grass
And hang zigzag on hedges. Green as glass
The water in the horse-trough shines.
Nine ducks go wobbling by in two straight lines.

A hen stares at nothing with one eye,
Then picks it up. Out of an empty sky
A swallow falls and, flickering through
The barn, dives up again into the dizzy blue.

I lie, not thinking, in the cool, soft grass,
Afraid of where a thought might take me – as
This grasshopper with plated face
Unfolds his legs and finds himself in space.

Self under self, a pile of selves I stand
Threaded on time, and with metaphysic hand
Lift the farm like a lid and see
Farm within farm, and in the centre, me.

NORMAN MacCAIG

26 Merritt Parkway

Motorway

    As if it were
forever that they move, that we
    keep moving –

        Under a wan sky where
        as the lights went on a star
            pierced the haze & now
        follows steadily
            a constant
        above our six lanes
        the dreamlike continuum . . .

And the people – ourselves !
  the humans from inside the
  cars, apparent
  only at gasoline stops
                  unsure,
      eyeing each other

                drink coffee hastily at the
          slot machines & hurry
      back to the cars
        vanish
        into them forever, to
        keep moving –

Houses now & then beyond the
sealed road, the trees/trees, bushes
passing by, passing
    the cars that
        keep moving ahead of
    us, past us, pressing behind us
               and
          over left, those that come
      toward us shining too brightly
moving relentlessly

   in six lanes, gliding
north & south, speeding with
a slurred sound –

DENISE LEVERTOV

27 Ballade

So much the goat scratches he can't sleep,
So much the pot takes water it breaks,
So much you heat iron it turns red,
So much you hammer it it cracks,
So much a man's worth as he's esteemed,
So much is he away he's forgotten,
So much is he bad he's despised,
So much you cry Noël that it comes.

So much you talk you contradict yourself,
So much fame's worth as it gets you favors,
So much you promise you take it back,
So much you beg you're given what you sought,
So much a thing's expensive everyone wants it,
So much you go after it you get it,
So much it's common it loses its charm,
So much you cry Noël that it comes.

So much you love a dog you feed it,
So much a song's heard it catches on,
So much fruit's hoarded up it goes rotten,
So much you dispute a place it's already taken,
So much you dawdle you ruin your life,
So much you hurry you run out of luck,
So much you hold on you lose your grip,
So much you cry Noël that it comes.

So much you joke you quit laughing,
So much you spend you lose your shirt,
So much you're honest you go broke,
So much is 'here' worth as a thing promised,
So much you love God you go to church,
So much you give you're obliged to borrow,
So much the wind shifts it blows cold at last,
So much you cry Noël that it comes.

Prince, so much a fool lives he wises up,
So much he travels he comes back home,
So much they beat him he knows he was wrong,
So much you cry Noël that it comes.

FRANÇOIS VILLON Translated from the French by Galway Kinnell

28 The Debate Between Villon's Heart and Body

Who's that I hear? *It's me. Who? Your heart,*
That hangs on only by a tiny thread.
It takes away my strength, substance and sap,
To see you withdrawn this way all alone
Like a whipped cur sulking in a corner.
Why is it, because of your lust for pleasure?
What's it to you? *I get the displeasure.*
Let me alone. *Why?* I'll give you an answer.
When will you do that? When I've grown up.
I've nothing more to say. I'll manage without it.

What do you have in mind? To get somewhere.
You're thirty, a lifetime for a mule,
And you call that childhood? No. *Then madness*
Has hold of you. By what, the collar?
You don't know anything. Yes I do. *What?* Flies in milk,
One's white, one's black, that's the difference.
And that's it? What do you want, an argument?
If that's not enough I'll begin again.
You're lost. I'll go down fighting.
I've nothing more to say. I'll manage without it.

I get the heartache, you the harm and pain.
If you were just some poor mixed-up nitwit
I'd be able to make excuses for you,
But you don't care, it's all one to you, foul or fair,
Either your head's harder than a rock
Or else you actually prefer misery to honor,
How do you answer this argument?
As soon as I'm dead it won't bother me.
God, what comfort. And what wise eloquence.
I've nothing more to say. I'll manage without it.

Where do your troubles come from? From bad luck,
When Saturn packed my bags for me
I guess he slipped in these woes. *That's insane.*
You're his lord and you act like his slave.
Look what Solomon wrote in his book,
'A wise man,' he says, 'has authority
Over the planets and their influence.'
I don't believe it, as they made me I'll be.

31

What are you saying? Just so, that's what I believe.
I've nothing more to say. I'll manage without it.

You want to live? God give me the strength.
You need . . . What? To feel penitent,
Read endlessly. Read in what? *Philosophy,*
And shun fools. I'll take your advice.
Then remember it. I have it fixed in mind.
Don't wait until you turn from bad to worse.
I've nothing more to say. I'll manage without it.

FRANÇOIS VILLON Translated from the French by. Galway Kinnell

29 The Nose

The nose grows during the whole of one's life.
(From scientific sources)

Yesterday my doctor told me:
'Clever you may be, however
Your snout is frozen.'
So don't go out in the cold,
Nose!

On me, on you, on Capuchin monks,
According to well-known medical laws,
Relentless as clocks, without pause
Nose-trunks triumphantly grow.

During the night they grow
On every citizen, high or low,
On janitors, ministers, rich and poor,
Hooting endlessly like owls,
Chilly and out of kilter,
Brutally bashed by a boxer
Or foully crushed by a door,
And those of our feminine neighbors
Are foxily screwed like drills
Into many a keyhole.

Gogol, that mystical uneasy soul,
Intuitively sensed their role.

My good friend Buggins got drunk: in his dream

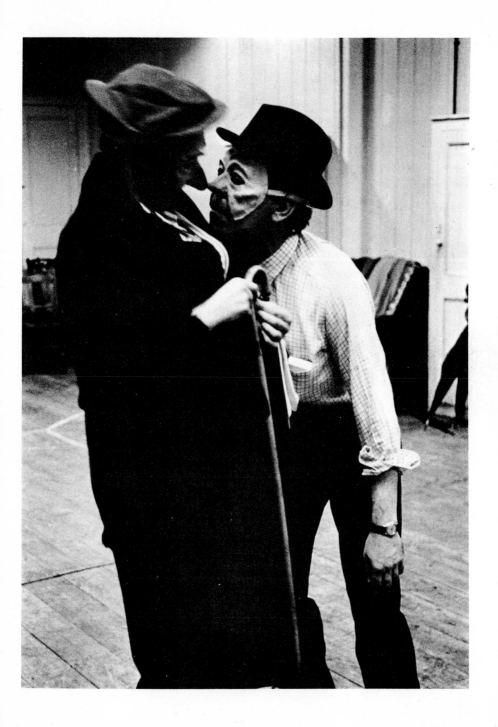

It seemed that, like a church spire
Breaking through washbowls and chandeliers,
Piercing and waking startled ceilings,
Impaling each floor like
Receipts on a spike,
Higher and higher

        rose

          his nose.

'What could that mean?' he wondered next morning.
'A warning,' I said, 'of Doomsday: it looks
As if they were going to check your books.'
On the 30th poor Buggins was haled off to jail.

Why, O Prime Mover of Noses, why
Do our noses grow longer, our lives shorter,
Why during the night should these fleshly lumps,
Like vampires or suction pumps,
Drain us dry?

They report that Eskimos
Kiss with their nose.

Among us this has not caught on.

ANDREI VOZNESENSKY Translated from the Russian by W. H. Auden

30 Where Are You Now, Batman?

Where are you now, Batman? Now that Aunt Heriot has
    reported Robin missing
And Superman's fallen asleep in the sixpenny childhood seats?
Where are you now that Captain Marvel's SHAZAM! echoes
    round the auditorium,
The magicians don't hear it,
Must all be deaf . . . or dead . . .
The Purple Monster who came down from the Purple Planet
    disguised as a man
Is wandering aimlessly about the streets
With no way of getting back.
Sir Galahad's been strangled by the Incredible Living Trees,
Zorro killed by his own sword.

Blackhawk has buried the last of his companions
And has now gone off to commit suicide in the disused
   Hangars of Innocence.
The Monster and the Ape still fight it out in a room
Where the walls are continually closing in;
Rocketman's fuel tanks gave out over London.
Even Flash Gordon's lost, he wanders among the stars
Weeping over the woman he loved
7 Universes ago.
        My celluloid companions, it's only a few years
Since I knew you. Something in us has faded.
        Has the Terrible Fiend, That Ghastly Adversary,
Mr Old Age, Caught you in his deadly trap,
And come finally to polish you off,
His machinegun dripping with years . . . ?

BRIAN PATTEN

31 A Day with the Foreign Legion

On one of those days with the Legion
When everyone sticks to sofas
And itches and bitches – a day
For gin and bitters and the plague –
Down by Mount Tessala, under the plane trees,
Seated at iron tables, cursing the country,
Cursing the times and the natives, cursing the drinks,
Cursing the food and the bugs, cursing the Legion,
Were Kim and Bim and all those brave
Heroes of all those books and plays and movies
The remorseless desert serves.
And as they sat at the iron tables cursing the country,
Cursing the food and the bugs, cursing the Legion,
Some Sergeant or other rushed in from The Fort
Gallantly bearing the news
From which all those the remorseless desert serves
Take their cues:
'Sir!'
        'What is it, Sergeant?'
                        'Sir, the hordes
March e'en now across the desert swards.'

Just like the movies.

Now in the movies
The Sergeant's arrival touches off bugles and bells,
Emptying bunks and showers, frightening horses,
Pushing up flags and standards, hardening lines
Of unsoldierly softness, and putting farewells
Hastily in the post so two weeks hence
A perfectly lovely lovely in far-off Canada
Will go pale and bite buttons and stare at the air in Canada.
And in the movies,
Almost before the audience spills its popcorn,
The company's formed and away, with Bim or Kim
Solemnly leading them out into a sandstorm
Getting them into what is quite clearly a trap,
Posting a double guard,
Sending messengers frantic to Marrakech,
Inadvertently pouring the water away,
Losing the ammunition, horses and food,
And generally carrying on in the great tradition
By making speeches
Which bring back to mind the glorious name of the Legion,
And serve as the turning point,
After which the Arabs seem doped and perfectly helpless,
Water springs up from the ground, the horses come back,
Plenty of food is discovered in some old cave,
And reinforcements arrive led by the girl
From Canada.

But in this instance nothing from *Beau Geste*
Or the Paramount lot was attempted,
It being too hot, too terribly hot, for dramatics
Even from Kim and Bim
Ageing under the plane trees,
Cursing the food and the bugs, cursing the Sergeant
Who gallantly bore the news because he was young,
Full of oats and ignorance, so damned young
In his pretty khaki; nothing at all,
So late in the day, with everyone crocked
And bitten to death and sweaty and all,
Was attempted despite the Sergeant,
Who whirled on his heel, his mission accomplished, and
     marched,

Hip hip,
Out of the bar, a true trooper, as if to the wars.

So the lights went on and the audience,
Pleasantly stupid, whistled and clapped at the rarity
Of a film breaking down in this late year of Our Lord.
But of course it was not the film; it was not the projector;
Nor was it the man in the booth, who hastened away
As soon as the feature was over, leaving the heroes
Cursing the food and the bugs, cursing the Legion
As heathendom marched and the Sergeant whirled, hip hip;
But some other, darker cause having to do
With the script perhaps, or the art.
Or not art –
None of these but still deeper, deeper and darker,
Rooted in Culture or . . . Culture, or . . .

Or none of these things. Or all.

What was it?

None of these things, or all. It was the time,
The time and the place, and how could one blame them,
Seated at iron tables cursing the country?
What could they do,
Seated under the plane trees watching the Sergeant
Whirl on his heel, hip hip, in his pretty khaki?
What could they say,
Drinking their gin and bitters by Mount Tessala,
What could they say?

For what after all *could* be said,
After all was said,
But that the feature had merely run out, and the lights had
    gone on
Because it was time for the lights to go on, and time
For them not to dash out in the desert,
But to rage
As befitted their age
At the drinks and the country, letting their audience
Clap, stamp, whistle and hoot as darkness
Settled on Mount Tessala, the lights went on,
The enemy roamed the desert, and everyone itched.

REED WHITTEMORE

32　Chief Standing Water

or *My Night on the Reservation*

Chief Standing Water
explained it

all to me –
the way he

left the reservation
(he was the only

Indian I ever
knew who

favoured explanation
explanation)

then his
conversion

(*Jesus Saves
Courtesy pays* –

the house
was full of texts)

and his
reversion to

'the ways of my people'
though he had

never (as he said)
forfeited

what civilization
taught him –

the house
was full of books

books like *The Book
of Mormon*

a brochure
on the Coronation

a copy of Blavatsky
(left by a former guest)

– her *Secret Doctrine*:
had he

read it? Oh he
had read

it. I like
my reading

heavy
he said:

he played
his drum

to a song
one hundred thousand

years old –
it told

the way his people
had come

from Yucatan
it predicted

the white-man:
you heard

words
like

Don't know
O.K.

embedded in
the archaic line

quite dis-
tinctly

and listen
he said

there's *Haircut*
and he sang it

again and look
my hair

is cut :
how's that now

for one hundred thousand
years ago

the archaeologists
don't-know-

nothin : and
in farewell :

this is not
he said

a motel but
Mrs Water and me

we
have our

plans for one
and the next

time that
you come

maybe . . .
I paid

the bill
and considering

the texts
they lived by

he and
Mrs Water

it was a
trifle high

*(Jesus pays
Courtesy saves)*

and that was my
night

on the
reservation.

CHARLES TOMLINSON

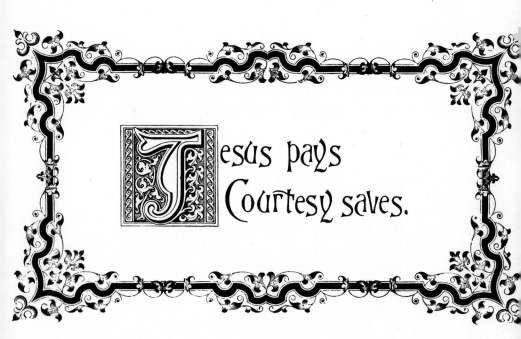

33 Judgements

I accuse –
    Ellen : you have become forty years old,
    and successful, tall, well-groomed,
    gracious, thoughtful, a secretary.
    Ellen, I accuse.

George –
    You know how to help others ;
    you manage a school. You never
    let fear or pride or faltering plans
    break your control.
    George, I accuse.

I accuse –
    Tom : you have found a role ;
    now you meet all kinds of people
    and let them find the truth of your
    eminence ; you need not push.
    Oh, Tom, I do accuse.

Remember –
    The gawky, hardly to survive students
    we were : not one of us going to succeed,
    all of us abjectly aware of how cold,
    unmanageable the real world was ?
    I remember. And that fear was true.
    And is true.

Last I accuse –
    Myself : my terrible poise, knowing
    even this, knowing that then we
    sprawled in the world
    and were ourselves part of it ; now
    we hold it firmly away with gracious
    gestures (like this of mine !) we've achieved.

I see it all too well –
    And I am accused, and I accuse.

WILLIAM STAFFORD

34 Pass Office Song

The scene is any pass office, where all male Africans must go to get their Registration Certificates. There they may wait in queues for hours and sometimes for days before they are attended to. It is a regulation which rankles in their minds and so they sing about it.

Take off your hat.
What is your home name?
Who is your father?
Who is your chief?
Where do you pay your tax?
What river do you drink?
We mourn for our country.

ANONYMOUS Transcribed by Peggy Rutherfoord

35 From William Tyndale to John Frith

The letters I, your lone friend, write in sorrow
Will not contain my sorrow: it is mine,
Not yours who stand for burning in my place.
Be certain of your fate. Though some, benign,
Will urge by their sweet threats, malicious love
And counsel dangerous fear of violence,
Theirs is illusion's goodness proving fair –
Against your wisdom – worldly innocence
And just persuasions' old hypocrisy.
Making their choice, reflect what you become:
Horror and misery bringing ruin where
The saintly mind has treacherously gone numb;
Despair in the deceit of your remorse
As, doubly heretic, you waste your past
Recanting, by all pitied, honourless,
Until you choose more easy death at last.
Think too of me. Sometimes in morning dark
I let my candle gutter and sit here
Brooding, as shadows fill my cell and sky
Breaks pale outside my window; then the dear

Companionship we spent working for love
Compels me to achieve a double portion.
In spite of age, insanity, despair,
Grief, or declining powers, we have done
What passes to the living of all men
Beyond our weariness. The fire shall find
Me hidden here, although its pain be less
If you have gone to it with half my mind,
Leaving me still enough to fasten flesh
Against the stake, flesh absolute with will.
And should your human powers and my need
Tremble at last and grow faint, worn, and ill,
Pain be too much to think of, fear destroy,
And animal reluctance from the womb,
Endurance of your end's integrity,
Be strong in this : heaven shall be your tomb.

(John Frith, Tyndale's most loyal disciple, returned to England
from the Continent in 1533, when he was thirty years old. He was
arrested and burned at the stake. This letter would have been
written to Frith in prison from Tyndale in Holland, where, not
long after, he too was imprisoned and burned at the stake for
heresy.)

EDGAR BOWERS

36 A Living

A man should never earn his living,
if he earns his life he'll be lovely.

A bird
picks up its seeds or little snails
between heedless earth and heaven
in heedlessness.

But, the plucky little sport, it gives to life
song, and chirruping, gay feathers, fluff-shadowed warmth
and all the unspeakable charm of birds hopping and fluttering
   and being birds.
– And we, we get it all from them for nothing.

D. H. LAWRENCE

37 What Is He?

What is he?
– A man, of course.
Yes, but what does he do?
– He lives and is a man.
Oh quite! but he must work. He must have a job of some sort.
– Why?
Because obviously he's not one of the leisured classes.
– I don't know. He has lots of leisure. And he makes quite
   beautiful chairs. –
There you are then! He's a cabinet maker.
– No no!
Anyhow a carpenter and joiner.
– Not at all.
But you said so.
– What did I say?
That he made chairs, and was a joiner and carpenter.
– I said he made chairs, but I did not say he was a carpenter.
All right then, he's just an amateur.
– Perhaps! Would you say a thrush was a professional flautist,
   or just an amateur? –
I'd say it was just a bird.
– And I say he is just a man.
All right! You always did quibble.

D. H. LAWRENCE

38 He Was

a brown old man with a green thumb:
I can remember the screak on stones of his hoe,
The chug, choke, and high madrigal wheeze
Of the spray-cart bumping below
The sputtery leaves of the apple trees,
But he was all but dumb

Who filled some quarter of the day with sound
All of my childhood long. For all I heard
Of all his labors, I can now recall
Never a single word
Until he went in the dead of fall
To the drowsy underground,

Having planted a young orchard with so great care
In that last year that none was lost, and May
Aroused them all, the leaves saying the land's
Praise for the livening clay,
And the found voice of his buried hands
Rose in the sparrowy air.

RICHARD WILBUR

39 Angry Samson

Are they blind, the lords of Gaza
  In their strong towers,
Who declare Samson pillow-smothered
  And stripped of his powers?

O stolid Philistines,
  Stare now in amaze
At my foxes running in your cornfields
  With their tails ablaze,

At swung jaw-bone, at bees swarming
  In the stark lion's hide,
At these, the gates of well-walled Gaza
  A-clank to my stride.

ROBERT GRAVES

40 Anecdote from Talk

John Watson was a tin-mine man
  An expert of his kind.
He worked up country in Malaya
  On whisky, not resigned,
  On whisky but not blind.

He told a friend he felt like death,
  And what you say's repeated.
The manager says 'I just sent for him
  With "Here's ten dollars, beat it

For Christ's sake to Singapore.
  I'm glad to pay the fare.
Just think of the nuisance, man, for me,
  If you pass out here."

Next day John Watson tapped the door
  With "Right, take my gun.
You've changed my mind, I mean to live."
  "I'll keep any gun.
  But I'll keep no madman."

This is the funny part,' the manager says,
  'He was shot just the same.
Of course I had to pass him to a dickey job.
  Just the natives, no-one to blame.
  But it was quick how it came.
  Three weeks.'

WILLIAM EMPSON

41 My Busconductor

My busconductor tells me
he only has one kidney
and that may soon go on strike
through overwork.
Each busticket

takes on now a different shape
and texture.
He holds a ninepenny single
as if it were a rose
and puts the shilling in his bag
as a child into a gasmeter.
His thin lips
have no quips
for fat factorygirls
and he ignores
the drunk who snores
and the oldman who talks to himself
and gets off at the wrong stop.
He goes gently to the bedroom
of the bus
to collect
and watch familiar shops and pubs passby
(perhaps for the last time?)
The sameold streets look different now
more distinct
as through new glasses.
And the sky
was it ever so blue?

And all the time
deepdown in the deserted busshelter of his mind
he thinks about his journey nearly done.
One day he'll clock on and never clock off
or clock off and never clock on.

ROGER McGOUGH

42 Bullocky

Beside his heavy-shouldered team,
thirsty with drought and chilled with rain,
he weathered all the striding years
till they ran widdershins in his brain:

Till the long solitary tracks
etched deeper with each lurching load
were populous before his eyes,
and fiends and angels used his road.

All the long straining journey grew
a mad apocalyptic dream,
and he old Moses, and the slaves
his suffering and stubborn team.

Then in his evening camp beneath
the half-light pillars of the trees
he filled the steepled cone of night
with shouted prayers and prophecies

While past the camp-fire's crimson ring
the star-struck darkness cupped him round,
and centuries of cattlebells
rang with their sweet uneasy sound.

Grass is across the waggon-tracks,
and plough strikes bone beneath the grass,
and vineyards cover all the slopes
where the dead teams were used to pass.

O vine, grow close upon that bone
and hold it with your rooted hand.
The prophet Moses feeds the grape,
and fruitful is the Promised Land.

JUDITH WRIGHT

43   Elegy for Alfred Hubbard

Hubbard is dead, the old plumber;
who will mend our burst pipes now,
the tap that has dripped all the summer,
testing the sink's overflow?

No other like him. Young men with knowledge
of new techniques, theories from books,

may better his work straight from college,
but who will challenge his squint-eyed looks

in kitchen, bathroom, under floorboards,
rules of thumb which were often wrong;
seek as erringly stopcocks in cupboards,
or make a job last half as long?

back alleys   He was a man who knew the ginnels,
alleyways, streets – the whole district,
family secrets, minor annals,
time-honoured fictions fused to fact.

Seventy years of gossip muttered
under his cap, his tufty thatch,
so that his talk was slow and clotted,
hard to follow, and too much.

As though nothing fell, none vanished,
and time were the maze of Cheetham Hill,
in which the dead – with jobs unfinished –
waited to hear him ring the bell.

For much he never got round to doing,
but meant to, when weather bucked up,
or worsened, or when his pipe was drawing,
or when he'd finished this cup.

I thought time, he forgot so often,
had forgotten him, but here's Death's pomp
over his house, and by the coffin
the son who will inherit his blowlamp,

tools, workshop, cart, and cornet
(pride of Cheetham Prize Brass Band),
and there's his mourning widow, Janet,
stood at the gate he'd promised to mend.

Soon he will make his final journey;
shaved and silent, strangely trim,
with never a pause to talk to any-
body: how arrow-like, for him!

In St Mark's Church, whose dismal tower
he pointed and painted when a lad,
they will sing his praises amidst flowers
while, somewhere, a cellar starts to flood,

and the housewife banging his front-door knocker
is not surprised to find him gone,
and runs for Thwaite, who's a better worker,
and sticks at a job until it's done.

TONY CONNOR

44 Elegy for Simon Corl, Botanist

With wildflowers bedded in his mind,
My blind great-uncle wrote a book.
His lips and beard were berry-stained,
Wrist broken like a shepherd's crook.

His door leaned open to the flies,
And May, like tendrils, wandered in.
The earth rose gently to his knees;
The clouds moved closer than his skin.

Sun against ear, he heard the slight
Stamen and pistil touch for days,
Felt pollen cast aslant like light
Into the shadows of his eyes.

When autumn stalked the leaves, he curled;
His fingers ripened like the sky;
His ink ran to a single word,
And the straight margin went awry.

When frost lay bristling on the weeds,
He smoothed it with a yellow thumb,
Followed his white cane to the woods
Between the saxifrage and thyme,

And heard the hornets crack like ice,
Felt worms arch backward in the snow;
And while the mites died under moss,
The clean scar sang across his brow.

DAVID WAGONER

Ben Shahn

45 Beautiful Old Age

It ought to be lovely to be old
to be full of the peace that comes of experience
and wrinkled ripe fulfilment.

The wrinkled smile of completeness that follows a life
lived undaunted and unsoured with accepted lies.
If people lived without accepting lies
they would ripen like apples, and be scented like pippins
in their old age.

Soothing, old people should be, like apples
when one is tired of love.
Fragrant like yellowing leaves, and dim with the soft
stillness and satisfaction of autumn.

And a girl should say:
It must be wonderful to live and grow old.
Look at my mother, how rich and still she is! –

And a young man should think: By Jove
my father has faced all weathers, but it's been a life! –

D. H. LAWRENCE

46 Sair Fyeld, Hinny

Sadly Fallen off,
Old Friend

knew

Sair fyeld, hinny, sair fyeld now,
Sair fyeld, hinny, since I kenned thou.

I was young and lusty, I was fair and clear;
I was young and lusty, many a long year.

When I was five and twenty, I was brave and bold;
But now I'm five and sixty, I'm both stiff and cold.

Thus spoke the old man to the oak tree:
Sair fyeld is I, since I kenned thee.

TRADITIONAL

47 Courage

What makes people unsatisfied
is that they accept lies.

If people had courage, and refused lies
and found out what they really felt and really meant
and acted on it,

They would distil the essential oil out of every experience
and like hazel-nuts in autumn, at last
be sweet and sound.

And the young among the old
would be as in the hazel-woods of September
nutting, gathering nuts of ripe experience.

As it is, all that the old can offer
is sour, bitter fruits, cankered by lies.

D. H. LAWRENCE

48 Room for a Blade of the Town

Room, room for a Blade of the Town
    That takes delight in roaring,
And daily rambles up and down
    And at night in the street lies snoring:

That for the noble name of Spark
    Dares his companions rally;
Commits an outrage in the dark,
    Then slinks into an alley.

To every female that he meets
    He swears he bears affection,
Defies all laws, arrests, and cheats
    By help of her protection:

Then he, intending further wrongs,
dupe, simpleton   By some resenting cully
Is decently run through the lungs,
    And there's an end of bully.

JOHN WILMOT, SECOND EARL OF ROCHESTER

49 Soup

I saw a famous man eating soup.
I say he was lifting a fat broth
Into his mouth with a spoon.
His name was in the newspapers that day
Spelled out in tall black headlines
And thousands of people were talking about him.

When I saw him,
He sat bending his head over a plate
Putting soup in his mouth with a spoon.

CARL SANDBURG

50 Epitaph on a Tyrant

Perfection, of a kind, was what he was after,
And the poetry he invented was easy to understand;
He knew human folly like the back of his hand,
And was greatly interested in armies and fleets;
When he laughed, respectable senators burst with laughter,
And when he cried the little children died in the streets.

W. H. AUDEN

51 Leader of Men

When he addressed ten thousand
Faces worked by automation
He was filled, exalted, afflated
With love and ambition for
His fellowcountrymen – in so far,
Of course,
As they were not incompatible
With the love and ambition he felt
For himself. No sacrifice
Would be too great. No
Holocaust. No bloodbath. He

Was affected by the nobility
Of his vision, his eyes were,
Naturally, blurred.

How was he to know
The mindless face of the crowd
Broke up, when he finished, into
Ten thousand pieces – except that,
When he went home,
He found the tea cold, his wife
Plain, his dogs smelly?

NORMAN MacCAIG

52 A Sane Revolution

If you make a revolution, make it for fun,
don't make it in ghastly seriousness,
don't do it in deadly earnest,
do it for fun.

Don't do it because you hate people,
do it just to spit in their eye.

Don't do it for the money,
do it and be damned to the money.

Don't do it for equality,
do it because we've got too much equality
and it would be fun to upset the apple-cart
and see which way the apples would go a-rolling.

Don't do it for the working classes.
Do it so that we can all of us be little aristocracies on our own
and kick our heels like jolly escaped asses.

Don't do it, anyhow, for international Labour.
Labour is the one thing a man has had too much of.
Let's abolish labour, let's have done with labouring!
Work can be fun, and men can enjoy it; then it's not labour.
Let's have it so! Let's make a revolution for fun!

D. H. LAWRENCE

53 Footnote to John ii, 4

Don't throw your arms around me in that way:
    I know that what you tell me is the truth –
    yes I suppose I loved you in my youth
    as boys do love their mothers, so they say,
    but all that's gone from me this many a day:
    I am a merciless cactus an uncouth
    wild goat a jagged old spear the grim tooth
    of a lone crag . . . Woman I cannot stay

Each one of us must do his work of doom
    and I shall do it even in despite
    of her who brought me in pain from her womb,
    whose blood made me, who used to bring the light
    and sit on the bed up in my little room
    and tell me stories and tuck me up at night.

R. A. K. MASON

54 Jesus and his Mother

My only son, more God's than mine,
Stay in this garden ripe with pears.
The yielding of their substance wears
A modest and contented shine:
And when they weep with age, not brine
But lazy syrup are their tears.
'I am my own and not my own.'

He seemed much like another man,
That silent foreigner who trod
Outside my door with lily rod:
How could I know what I began
Meeting the eyes more furious than
The eyes of Joseph, those of God?
I was my own and not my own.

And who are these twelve labouring men?
I do not understand your words:
I taught you speech, we named the birds,
You marked their big migrations then
Like any child. So turn again
To silence from the place of crowds,
'I am my own and not my own.'

Why are you sullen when I speak?
Here are your tools, the saw and knife
And hammer on your bench. Your life
Is measured here in week and week
Planed as the furniture you make,
And I will teach you like a wife
To be my own and all my own.

Who like an arrogant wind blown
Where he may please, needs no content?
Yet I remember how you went
To speak with scholars in furred gown.
I hear an outcry in the town;
Who carries that dark instrument?
'One all his own and not his own.'

Treading the green and nimble sward
I stare at a strange shadow thrown.
Are you the boy I bore alone
No doctor near to cut the cord?
I cannot reach to call you Lord,
Answer me as my only son.
'I am my own and not my own.'

THOM GUNN

55 Ballad of the Bread Man

Mary stood in the kitchen
Baking a loaf of bread.
An angel flew in through the window.
We've a job for you, he said.

God in his big gold heaven,
Sitting in his big blue chair,
Wanted a mother for his little son.
Suddenly saw you there.

Mary shook and trembled,
It isn't true what you say.
Don't say that, said the angel.
The baby's on its way.

Joseph was in the workshop
Planing a piece of wood.
The old man's past it, the neighbours said.
That girl's been up to no good.

And who was that elegant feller,
They said, in the shiny gear?
The things they said about Gabriel
Were hardly fit to hear.

Mary never answered,
Mary never replied.
She kept the information,
Like the baby, safe inside.

It was election winter.
They went to vote in town.
When Mary found her time had come
The hotels let her down.

The baby was born in an annex
Next to the local pub.
At midnight, a delegation
Turned up from the Farmer's Club.

They talked about an explosion
That cracked a hole in the sky,
Said they'd been sent to the Lamb & Flag
To see god come down from on high.

A few days later a bishop
And a five-star general were seen
With the head of an African country
In a bullet-proof limousine.

We've come, they said, with tokens
For the little boy to choose.
Told the tale about war and peace
In the television news.

After them came the soldiers
With rifle and bomb and gun,
Looking for enemies of the state.
The family had packed and gone.

When they got back to the village
The neighbours said to a man,
That boy will never be one of us,
Though he does what he blessed well can.

He went round to all the people
A paper crown on his head.
Here is some bread from my father.
Take, eat, he said.

Nobody seemed very hungry,
Nobody seemed to care.
Nobody saw the god in himself
Quietly standing there.

He finished up in the papers.
He came to a very bad end.
He was charged with bringing the living to life.
No man was that prisoner's friend.

There's only one kind of punishment
To fit that kind of a crime.
They rigged a trial and shot him dead.
They were only just in time.

if you must have sherry with your bitters,
if money and fame are your pigeon,
if you feel that you need success
and long for a good address,
don't anchor here in the desert –
the fishing isn't so good :
take a ticket for Megalopolis,
don't stay in this neighbourhood !

A. R. D. FAIRBURN

57 Don't Sign Anything

Riding the horse as was my wont,
there was a bunch of cows in a field.

The horse
chased

them. I likewise, an uneasy
accompanist.

To wit, the Chinese proverb goes :
if you lie in a field

and fall asleep,
you will be found in a field

asleep.

ROBERT CREELEY

58 Paradise

I blesse thee, Lord, because I GROW
Among thy trees, which in a ROW
To thee both fruit and order OW.

What open force, or hidden CHARM
Can blast my fruit, or bring me HARM,
While the inclosure is thine ARM ?

They lifted the young man by the leg,
They lifted him by the arm,
They locked him in a cathedral
In case he came to harm.

They stored him safe as water
Under seven rocks.
One Sunday morning he burst out
Like a jack-in-the-box.

Through the town he went walking.
He showed them the holes in his head.
Now do you want any loaves? he cried.
Not today, they said.

CHARLES CAUSLEY

56 I'm Older than You, Please Listen

To the young man I would say:
Get out! Look sharp, my boy,
before the roots are down,
before the equations are struck,
before a face or a landscape
has power to shape or destroy.
This land is a lump without leaven,
a body that has no nerves.
Don't be content to live in
a sort of second-grade heaven
with first-grade butter, fresh air,
and paper in every toilet;
becoming a butt for the malice
of those who have stayed and soured,
staying in turn to sour,
to smile, and savage the young.
If you're enterprising and able,
smuggle your talents away,
hawk them in livelier markets
where people are willing to pay.
If you have no stomach for roughage,
if patience isn't your religion,

Inclose me still for fear I START.
Be to me rather sharp and TART,
lack   Than let me want thy hand & ART.

When thou dost greater judgements SPARE,
And with thy knife but prune and PARE,
Ev'n fruitfull trees more fruitfull ARE.

Such sharpness shows the sweetest FREND :
Such cuttings rather heal than REND :
aim *or* terminus   And such beginnings touch their END.

GEORGE HERBERT

59 Brothers

How lovely the elder brother's
Life all laced in the other's,
Lóve-laced ! – what once I well
Witnessed ; so fortune fell.
When Shrovetide, two years gone,
Our boys' plays brought on
Part was picked for John,
Young Jóhn ; then fear, then joy
Ran revel in the elder boy.
Their night was come now ; all
Our company thronged the hall ;
Henry, by the wall,
Beckoned me beside him :
I came where called, and eyed him
By meanwhiles ; making mý play
Turn most on tender byplay.
For, wrung all on love's rack,
My lad, and lost in Jack,
Smiled, blushed, and bit his lip ;
Or drove, with a diver's dip,
Clutched hands down through clasped knees –
Truth's tokens tricks like these,
Old telltales, with what stress
He hung on the imp's success.
Now the other was bráss-bóld :

Hé had no work to hold
His heart up at the strain;
Nay, roguish ran the vein.
Two tedious acts were past;
Jack's call and cue at last;
When Henry, heart-forsook,
Dropped eyes and dared not look.
Eh, how áll rúng!
Young dog, he did give tongue!
But Harry – in his hands he has flung
His tear-tricked cheeks of flame
For fond love and for shame.
   Ah Nature, framed in fault,
There's comfort then, there's salt;
Nature, bad, base, and blind,
Dearly thou canst be kind;
There dearly thén, deárly,
I'll cry thou canst be kind.

GERARD MANLEY HOPKINS

60 Then my Love and I'll be Married

sulphur

When roses grow on thistle tops,
And brimstone's took for sugar candy,
And women can't eat sugar sops,
Oh, then my love and I'll be married.

When gold is thrown about the street,
And lies from June to January,
And dogs will not spare bones for meat,
Oh, then my love and I'll be married.

When a cobbler works without an awl,
And London into York is carried,
When smoke won't rise, nor water fall,
Oh, then my love and I'll be married.

TRADITIONAL

61 The Plot against the Giant

FIRST GIRL   When this yokel comes maundering,
                     Whetting his hacker,
                     I shall run before him,
                     Diffusing the civilest odours
                     Out of geraniums and unsmelled flowers.
                     It will check him.

SECOND GIRL   I shall run before him,
                     Arching cloths besprinkled with colours
                     As small as fish-eggs.
                     The threads
                     Will abash him.

THIRD GIRL   Oh, la . . . le pauvre !
                     I shall run before him,
                     With a curious puffing.
                     He will bend his ear then.
                     I shall whisper
                     Heavenly labials in a world of gutturals.
                     It will undo him.

WALLACE STEVENS

62 The Garden

Like a skein of loose silk blown against a wall
She walks by the railing of a path in Kensington Gardens,
And she is dying piece-meal of a sort of emotional anaemia.

And round about there is a rabble
Of the filthy, sturdy, unkillable infants of the very poor.
They shall inherit the earth.

In her is the end of breeding.
Her boredom is exquisite and excessive.
She would like some one to speak to her,
And is almost afraid that I will commit that indiscretion.

EZRA POUND

63 Father and Child

She hears me strike the board and say
That she is under ban
Of all good men and women,
Being mentioned with a man
That has the worst of all bad names;
And thereupon replies
That his hair is beautiful,
Cold as the March wind his eyes.

W. B. YEATS

64 Strawberries

There were never strawberries
like the ones we had
that sultry afternoon
sitting on the step
of the open french window
facing each other
your knees held in mine
the blue plates in our laps
the strawberries glistening
in the hot sunlight
we dipped them in sugar
looking at each other
not hurrying the feast
for one to come
the empty plates
laid on the stone together
with the two forks crossed
and I bent towards you
sweet in that air
in my arms
abandoned like a child
from your eager mouth
the taste of strawberries
in my memory
lean back again

let me love you
let the sun beat
on our forgetfulness
one hour of all
the heat intense
and summer lightning
on the Kilpatrick hills

let the storm wash the plates

EDWIN MORGAN

65 The Picnic

It is the picnic with Ruth in the spring.
Ruth was third on my list of seven girls
But the first two were gone (Betty) or else
Had someone (Ellen has accepted Doug).
Indian Gully the last day of school;
Girls make the lunches for the boys too.
I wrote a note to Ruth in algebra class
Day before the test. She smiled, and nodded.
We left the cars and walked through the young corn,
The shoots green as paint and the leaves like tongues
Trembling. Beyond the fence where we stood
Some wild strawberry flowered by an elm tree
And Jack-in-the-pulpit was olive ripe.
A blackbird fled as I crossed, and showed
A spot of gold or red under its quick wing.
I held the wire for Ruth and watched the whip
Of her long, striped skirt as she followed.
Three freckles blossomed on her thin, white back
Underneath the loop where the blouse buttoned.
We went for our lunch away from the rest,
Stretched in the new grass, our heads close
Over unknown things wrapped up in wax papers.
Ruth tried for the same, I forget what it was,
And our hands were together. She laughed,
And a breeze caught the edge of her little
Collar and the edge of her brown, loose hair

That touched my cheek. I turned my face in-
to the gentle fall. I saw how sweet it smelled.
She didn't move her head or take her hand.
I felt a soft caving in my stomach
As at the top of the highest slide
When I had been a child, but was not afraid,
And did not know why my eyes moved with wet
As I brushed her cheek with my lips and brushed
Her lips with my own lips. She said to me
Jack, Jack, different than I had ever heard,
Because she wasn't calling me, I think,
Or telling me. She used my name to
Talk in another way I wanted to know.
She laughed again and then she took her hand;
I gave her what we both had touched – can't
Remember what it was, and we ate the lunch.
Afterward we walked in the small, cool creek
Our shoes off, her skirt hitched, and she smiling,
My pants rolled, and then we climbed up the high
Side of Indian Gully and looked
Where we had been, our hands together again.
It was then some bright thing came in my eyes,
Starting at the back of them and flowing
Suddenly through my head and down my arms
And stomach and my bare legs that seemed not
To stop in feet, not to feel the red earth
Of the Gully, as though we hung in a
Touch of birds. There was a word in my throat
With the feeling and I knew the first time
What it meant and I said, it's beautiful.
Yes, she said, and I felt the sound and word
In my hand join the sound and word in hers
As in one name said, or in one cupped hand.
We put back on our shoes and socks and we
Sat in the grass awhile, crosslegged, under
A blowing tree, not saying anything.
And Ruth played with shells she found in the creek,
As I watched. Her small wrist which was so sweet
To me turned by her breast and the shells dropped
Green, white, blue, easily into her lap,
Passing light through themselves. She gave the pale

Shells to me, and got up and touched her hips
With her light hands, and we walked down slowly
To play the school games with the others.

JOHN LOGAN

66 Plucking the Rushes

A boy and girl are sent to gather rushes for thatching.
(Fourth or Fifth Century)

Green rushes with red shoots,
Long leaves bending to the wind –
You and I in the same boat
Plucking rushes at the Five Lakes.
We started at dawn from the orchid-island;
We rested under the elms till noon.
You and I plucking rushes
Had not plucked a handful when night came!

ANONYMOUS Translated from the Chinese by Arthur Waley

67 When Molly Smiles

When Molly smiles beneath her cow,
I feel my heart – I can't tell how;
When Molly is on Sunday dressed,
On Sundays I can take no rest.

What can I do? On working days
I leave my work on her to gaze.
What shall I say? At sermons, I
Forget the text when Molly's by.

Good master curate, teach me how
To mind your preaching and my plough:
And if for this you'll raise a spell,
A good fat goose shall thank you well.

ANONYMOUS

68 Love Will Find Out The Way

Over the mountains,
And over the waves;
Under the fountains,
And under the graves;
Under floods that are deepest
Which Neptune obey;
Over rocks that are steepest,
Love will find out the way.

Where there is no place
For the glow-worm to lie;
Where there is no space
For receipt of a fly;
Where the midge dares not venture
Lest herself fast she lay;
If love come, he will enter,
And soon find out his way.

You may esteem him
A child for his might;
Or you may deem him
A coward from his flight;
But if she, whom love doth honour,
Be concealed from the day,
Set a thousand guards upon her,
Love will find out the way.

Some think to lose him
By having him confined;
And some do suppose him,
Poor thing, to be blind;
But however close you wall him,
Do the best that you may,
Blind love, if so you call him,
Will find out his way.

You may train the eagle
To stoop to your fist;
Or you may inveigle
The phoenix of the east;
The lioness, you may move her
To give o'er her prey;
But you'll ne'er stop a lover:
He will find out his way.

TRADITIONAL

69 On a Painted Woman

To youths, who hurry thus away,
   How silly your desire is
At such an early hour to pay
   Your compliments to Iris.

Stop, prithee, stop, ye hasty beaux,
   No longer urge this race on;
Though Iris has put on her clothes,
   She has not put her face on.

GEORGES DE BREBEUF Translated from the French by Percy Bysshe Shelley

70 People Hide their Love

Who says that it's by my desire,
This separation, this living so far from you?
My dress still smells of the perfume that you wore;
My hand still holds the letter that you sent.
Round my waist I wear a double sash;
I dream that it binds us both with a same-heart knot.
Did you know that people hide their love,
Like a flower that seems too precious to be picked?

WU-TI Translated from the Chinese by Arthur Waley

71 The Sick Rose

O rose, thou art sick!
The invisible worm,
That flies in the night,
In the howling storm,

Has found out thy bed
Of crimson joy,
And his dark secret love
Does thy life destroy.

WILLIAM BLAKE

72 The Unquiet Grave

'The wind doth blow today, my love,
And a few small drops of rain;
I never had but one true love;
In cold grave she was lain.

I'll do as much for my true love
As any young man may;
I'll sit and mourn all at her grave
For a twelvemonth and a day.'

The twelvemonth and a day being up,
The dead began to speak:
'Oh who sits weeping on my grave,
And will not let me sleep?'

''Tis I, my love, sits on your grave,
And will not let you sleep;
For I crave one kiss of your clay-cold lips
And that is all I seek.'

'You crave one kiss of my clay-cold lips;
But my breath smells earthy strong;
If you have one kiss of my clay-cold lips,
Your time will not be long.

'Tis down in yonder garden green,
Love, where we used to walk,
The finest flower that ere was seen
Is withered to a stalk.

The stalk is withered dry, my love,
So will our hearts decay;
So make yourself content, my love,
Till death calls you away.'

TRADITIONAL

73 The Clock-Winder

It is dark as a cave,
Or a vault in the nave
When the iron door
Is closed, and the floor
Of the church relaid
With trowel and spade.

But the parish-clerk
Cares not for the dark
As he winds in the tower
At a regular hour
The rheumatic clock
Whose dilatory knock
You can hear when praying
At the day's decaying,
Or at any lone while
From a pew in the aisle.

Up, up from the ground
Around and around
In the turret stair
He clambers, to where
The wheelwork is,
With its tick, click, whizz,
Reposefully measuring
Each day to its end
That mortal men spend

In sorrowing and pleasuring.
Nightly thus does he climb
To the trackway of Time.

Him I followed one night
To this place without light,
And, ere I spoke, heard
Him say, word by word,
At the end of his winding,
The darkness unminding : –

'So I wipe out one more,
My Dear, of the sore
Sad days that still be,
Like a drying Dead Sea,
Between you and me !'

Who she was no man knew :
He had long borne him blind
To all womankind ;
And was ever one who
Kept his past out of view.

THOMAS HARDY

74 In my Craft or Sullen Art

In my craft or sullen art
Exercised in the still night
When only the moon rages
And the lovers lie abed
With all their griefs in their arms,
I labour by singing light
Not for ambition or bread
Or the strut and trade of charms
On the ivory stages
But for the common wages
Of their most secret heart.

Not for the proud man apart
From the raging moon I write
On these spindrift pages
Nor for the towering dead
With their nightingales and psalms
But for the lovers, their arms
Round the griefs of the ages,
Who pay no praise or wages
Nor heed my craft or art.

DYLAN THOMAS

75 Jazz Fantasia

Drum on your drums, batter on your banjoes,
sob on the long cool winding saxophones.
Go to it, O jazzmen.

Sling your knuckles on the bottoms of the happy
tin pans, let your trombones ooze, and go husha-
husha-hush with the slippery sand-paper.

Moan like an autumn wind high in the lonesome treetops,
    moan soft like
you wanted somebody terrible, cry like a racing car slipping
    away from a
motorcycle cop, bang-bang! you jazzmen, bang altogether
    drums, traps,
banjoes, horns, tin cans – make two people fight on the top
    of a stairway
and scratch each other's eyes in a clinch tumbling down the
    stairs.

Can the rough stuff . . . now a Mississippi steamboat pushes
    up the night
river with a hoo-hoo-hoo-oo . . . and the green lanterns
    calling to the high
soft stars . . . a red moon rides on the humps of the low
    river hills . . .
go to it, O jazzmen.

CARL SANDBURG

76 Ballad

A faithless shepherd courted me,
He stole away my liberty;
When my poor heart was strange to men
He came and smiled and stole it then.

When my apron would hang low
Me he sought through frost and snow;
When it puckered up with shame
And I sought him, he never came.

When summer brought no fears to fright,
He came to guard me every night;
When winter nights did darkly prove,
None came to guard me or to love.

I wish, I wish – but it's in vain –
I wish I was a maid again;
A maid again I cannot be:
O when will green grass cover me?

I wish my babe had ne'er been born;
I've made its pillow on a thorn.
I wish my sorrows all away,
My soul with God, my body clay.

He promised beds as fine as silk
And sheets for love as white as milk
But he when won my heart astray
Left me to want a bed of clay.

He kept his sheep on yonder hill,
His heart seemed soft but it was steel;
I ran with love and was undone,
O had I walked ere I did run.

He has two hearts and I have none;
He'll be a rogue, when I am gone,
To thee, my baby, unto thee,
As he has been too long to me.

I weep the past, I dread the gloom
Of sorrows in the time to come;
When thou without a friend shalt be
Weeping on a stranger's knee.

My heart would break – but it is brass –
To see thee smile upon my face,
To see thee smile at words that be
The messengers of grief to thee.

I wish, my child, thou'dst ne'er been born,
I've made thy pillow on a thorn;
I wish our sorrows both away,
Our souls with God, our bodies clay.

TRADITIONAL

77 Girls in a Factory

Seated in rows at the machines
Their heads are bent; the tacking needle
Stitches along the hours, along the seams.

What thoughts follow the needle
Over the fields of cloth,
Stitching into the seams
Perhaps a scarlet thread of love,
A daisy-chain of dreams?

DENIS GLOVER

78 Go By Brooks

Go by brooks, love,
Where fish stare,
Go by brooks,
I will pass there.

Go by rivers,
Where the eels throng,
Rivers, love,
I won't be long.

Go by oceans,
Where whales sail,
Oceans, love,
I will not fail.

LEONARD COHEN

79 A Thousand Years

A thousand years, you said,
As our hearts melted.
I look at the hand you held,
And the ache is hard to bear.

LADY HEGURI Translated from the Japanese by Geoffrey Bownas and
Anthony Thwaite

80 My Tangled Hair

My tangled hair
I shall not cut:
Your hand, my dearest,
Touched it as a pillow.

ANONYMOUS Translated from the Japanese by Geoffrey Bownas and
Anthony Thwaite

81 Cat-Goddesses

A perverse habit of cat-goddesses –
Even the blackest of them, black as coals
Save for a new moon blazing on each breast,
With coral tongues and beryl eyes like lamps,
Long-leggèd, pacing three by three in nines –
This obstinate habit is to yield themselves,
In verisimilar love-ecstasies,
To tatter-eared and slinking alley-toms
No less below the common run of cats
Than they above it; which they do for spite,
To provoke jealousy – not the least abashed
By such gross-headed, rabbit-coloured litters
As soon they shall be happy to desert.

ROBERT GRAVES

82 For Anne

With Annie gone,
Whose eyes to compare
With the morning sun?

Not that I did compare,
But I do compare
Now that she's gone.

LEONARD COHEN

83 Song

I'll come to thee at even tide
When the west is streaked wi grey
I'll wish the night thy charms to hide
And daylight all away

I'll come to thee at set o' sun
Where white thorns i' the May
I'll come to thee when work is done
And love thee till the day

When Daisey stars are all turned green
And all is meadow grass
grass strip I'll wander down the bauk at e'en
And court the bonny Lass

The green banks and the rustleing sedge
I'll wander down at e'en
All slopeing to the waters edge
And in the water green

And theres the luscious meadow sweet
Beside the meadow drain
My lassie there I once did meet
Who I wish to meet again

were The water lilies where in flower
The yellow and the white
I met her there at even's hour
And stood for half the night

We stood and loved in that green place
When sundays sun got low
Its beams reflected in her face
The fairest thing below

My sweet Ann Foot my bonny Ann
The Meadow banks are green
Meet me at even when you can
Be mine as you have been

JOHN CLARE

84 We'll Go No More A-roving

So, we'll go no more a-roving
    So late into the night,
Though the heart be still as loving
    And the moon be still as bright.

For the sword outwears its sheath,
    And the soul wears out the breast,
And the heart must pause to breathe,
    And love itself have rest.

Though the night was made for loving,
    And the day returns too soon,
Yet we'll go no more a-roving
    By the light of the moon.

LORD BYRON

85 The Royal Duke of Grantham

Six dukes went a-fishing
Down by yon seaside.
One of them spied a dead body
Come floating on the tide.

The one said to each other,
These words I heard them say:
''Tis the Royal Duke of Grantham
That the tide have washed away.'

They took him to London
To a place where he was known;
From there up the Humber
To the place where he was born.

Black is the mourning
And white is the wand,
And so yellow are the flamboys
That they carried in their hand.

processional cross
flaming torches

He now lies between two towers,
He lies in the blue clay.
And the Royal Queen of Grantham
Went weeping away.

TRADITIONAL

86 She's like the Swallow

She's like the swallow that flies so high,
She's like the river that never runs dry,
She's like the sunshine on the lee shore,
I love my love and love is no more.

'Twas out in the garden this fair maid did go,
A-picking the beautiful prim-e-rose;
The more she plucked the more she pulled
Until she got her a-per-on full.

It's out of the roses she made a bed,
A stony pillow for her head.
She laid her down, no word did say,
Until this fair maid's heart did break.

She's like the swallow that flies so high,
She's like the river that never runs dry,
She's like the sunshine on the lee shore,
I love my love and love is no more.

TRADITIONAL

87 To My Dear and Loving Husband

If ever two were one, then surely we.
If ever man were lov'd by wife, then thee.
If ever wife was happy in a man,
Compare with me, ye women, if you can.
I prize thy love more than whole mines of gold,
Or all the riches that the east doth hold.
My love is such that rivers cannot quench,
Nor ought but love from thee give recompence.
Thy love is such I can no way repay;
The heavens reward thee manifold I pray.
Then while we live, in love let's so perséver,
That when we live no more, we may live ever.

ANNE BRADSTREET

88 Sea Chest

There was a woman loved a man
as the man loved the sea.
Her thoughts of him were the same
as his thoughts of the sea.
They made an old sea chest for their belongings
together.

CARL SANDBURG

89 Frankie and Johnny

Frankie and Johnny were lovers,
Lordy, how they could love,
Swore to be true to each other,
True as the stars above,
  He was her man, but he done her wrong.

Little Frankie was a good gal,
As everybody knows,
She did all the work around the house,
And pressed her Johnny's clothes,
  He was her man, but he done her wrong.

Johnny was a yeller man,
With coal black, curly hair,
Everyone up in St Louis
Thought he was a millionaire,
  He was her man, but he done her wrong.

Frankie went down to the bar-room,
Called for a bottle of beer,
Says, 'Looky here, Mister Bartender,
Has my lovin' Johnny been here?
  He is my man, and he's doin' me wrong.'

'I will not tell you no story,
I will not tell you no lie.
Johnny left here about an hour ago,
With a gal named Nelly Bly,
  He is your man and he's doing you wrong.'

Little Frankie went down Broadway,
With her pistol in her hand,
Said, 'Stand aside you chorus gals,
I'm lookin' for my man,
  He is my man, and he's doin' me wrong.'

The first time she shot him, he staggered,
The next time she shot him, he fell,
The last time she shot, O Lawdy,
There was a new man's face in hell,
  She shot her man, for doin' her wrong.

'Turn me over doctor,
Turn me over slow,
I got a bullet in my left hand side,
Great God, it's hurtin' me so.
  I was her man, but I done her wrong.'

It was a rubber-tyred buggy,
Decorated hack,
Took poor Johnny to the graveyard,
Brought little Frankie back,
  He was her man, but he done her wrong.

It was not murder in the first degree,
It was not murder in the third,
A woman simply dropped her man
Like a hunter drops his bird,
  She shot her man, for doin' her wrong.

The last time I saw Frankie,
She was sittin' in the 'lectric chair,
Waitin' to go and meet her God
With the sweat runnin' out of her hair,
  She shot her man, for doin' her wrong.

Walked on down Broadway,
As far as I could see,
All I could hear was a two string bow
Playin' '*Nearer my God to ·thee*',
  He was her man, and he done her wrong.

TRADITIONAL AMERICAN

90 Ou Phrontis

TO E. M. FORSTER

The bells assault the maiden air,
The coachman waits with a carriage and pair,
But the bridegroom says *I won't be there*,
    I don't care!

Three times three times the banns declare
That the boys may blush and the girls may glare,
But the bridegroom is occupied elsewhere,
    I don't care!

Lord, but the neighbours all will stare,
Their temperatures jump as high as a hare,
But the bridegroom says *I've paid my fare*,
    I don't care!

The bride she waits by the bed so bare,
Soft as a pillow is her hair,
But the bridegroom jigs with the leg of a chair,
    I don't care!

Say, but her father's a millionaire,
A girdle of gold all night will she wear,
You must your foolish ways forswear.
    I don't care!

Her mother will offer, if she dare,
A ring that is rich but not so rare
If you'll keep your friendship in repair.
    I don't care!

Her sisters will give you a plum and a pear
And a diamond saddle for your mare.
O bridegroom! For the night prepare!
    I don't care!

Her seven brothers all debonair
Will do your wishes and some to spare
If from your fancy you'll forbear.
    I don't care!

Say, but a maid you wouldn't scare
Now that you've got her in your snare?
And what about your son and heir?
  I don't care!

She'll leap, she'll leap from the highest stair,
She'll drown herself in the river there,
With a silver knife her flesh she'll tear.
  I don't care!

Then another will lie in the silken lair
And cover with kisses her springing hair.
Another the bridal bed will share.
  I don't care!

I shall stand on my head on the table bare,
I shall kick my lily-white legs in the air,
I shall wash my hands of the whole affair,
  I don't care!

CHARLES CAUSLEY

91 On Thomas Bond and his Wife

Here lie the bodies
Of Thomas Bond, and Mary his wife.
She was temperate, chaste, charitable,
BUT
She was proud, peevish, and passionate.
She was an affectionate wife, and a tender mother;
BUT
Her husband and child, whom she loved,
Seldom saw her countenance without a disgusting
frown;
Whilst she received visitors, whom she despised,
With an endearing smile.
Her behaviour was discreet towards strangers,
BUT
Imprudent in her family.
Abroad, her conduct was influenced by good
breeding;

BUT

At home by ill temper.
She was a professed enemy to flattery,
And was seldom known to praise or commend;

BUT

The talents in which she principally excelled,
Were difference of opinion, and
Discovering flaws and imperfections.
She was an admirable economist,
And, without prodigality,
Dispensed plenty to every person in her family;

BUT

Would sacrifice their eyes to a farthing candle.
She sometimes made her husband happy
With her good qualities;

BUT

Much more frequently miserable,
With her many failings;
Insomuch, that in thirty years cohabitation,
He often lamented,
despite   That maugre all her virtues,
He had not, in the whole, enjoyed
Two years of matrimonial comfort.

AT LENGTH

Finding she had lost the affections of her husband,
As well as the regard of her neighbours,
Family disputes having been divulged by servants,
She died of vexation, July 20, 1768, aged 48.
Her worn-out husband survived her
Four months and two days,
And departed this life, Nov. 28, 1768, aged 54.
WILLIAM BOND, brother to the deceased,
Erected this stone,
As a *weekly monitor* to the surviving
Wives of this parish,
That they may avoid the infamy
Of having their memories handed down to posterity,
With a patchwork character.

ANONYMOUS (WILLIAM BOND?)

92 Passing Remark

In scenery I like flat country.
In life I don't like much to happen.

In personalities I like mild colorless people.
And in colors I prefer gray and brown.

My wife, a vivid girl from the mountains,
says, 'Then why did you choose me?'

Mildly I lower my brown eyes –
there are so many things admirable people do not understand.

WILLIAM STAFFORD

93 Love Comes Quietly

Love comes quietly,
finally, drops
about me, on me,
in the old ways.

What did I know
thinking myself
able to go
alone all the way.

ROBERT CREELEY

94 The Magpies

When Tom and Elizabeth took the farm
    The bracken made their bed,
And *Quardle oodle ardle wardle doodle*
    The magpies said.

Tom's hand was strong to the plough,
    Elizabeth's lips were red,
And *Quardle oodle ardle wardle doodle*
    The magpies said.

Year in year out they worked
    While the pines grew overhead,
And *Quardle oodle ardle wardle doodle*
    The magpies said.

But all the beautiful crops soon went
    To the mortgage-man instead,
And *Quardle oodle ardle wardle doodle*
    The magpies said.

Elizabeth is dead now (it's years ago),
    Old Tom went light in the head;
And *Quardle oodle ardle wardle doodle*
    The magpies said.

The farm's still there. Mortgage corporations
    Couldn't give it away.
And *Quardle oodle ardle wardle doodle*
    The magpies said.

DENIS GLOVER

95 Lovers in Winter

The posture of the tree
    Shows the prevailing wind;
And ours, long misery
    When you are long unkind.

But forward, look, we lean –
    Not backward as in doubt –
And still with branches green
    Ride our ill weather out.

ROBERT GRAVES

96 The Telephone

'When I was just as far as I could walk
From here today,
There was an hour
All still
When leaning with my head against a flower
I heard you talk.
Don't say I didn't, for I heard you say –
You spoke from that flower on the window sill –
Do you remember what it was you said?'

'First tell me what it was you thought you heard.'

'Having found the flower and driven a bee away,
I leaned my head,
And holding by the stalk,
I listened and I thought I caught the word –
What was it? Did you call me by my name?
Or did you say –
Someone said "Come" – I heard it as I bowed.'

'I may have thought as much, but not aloud.'

'Well, so I came.'

ROBERT FROST

97 Effort at Speech Between Two People

Speak to me.   Take my hand.   What are you now?
I will tell you all.   I will conceal nothing.
When I was three, a little child read a story about a rabbit
who died, in the story, and I crawled under a chair:
a pink rabbit: it was my birthday, and a candle
burnt a sore spot on my finger, and I was told to be happy.

Oh, grow to know me.   I am not happy.   I will be open:
Now I am thinking of white sails against a sky like music,
like glad horns blowing, and birds tilting, and an arm about me.
There was one I loved, who wanted to live, sailing.

Speak to me. Take my hand. What are you now?
When I was nine, I was fruitily sentimental,
fluid: and my widowed aunt played Chopin,
and I bent my head on the painted woodwork, and wept.
I want now to be close to you. I would
link the minutes of my days close, somehow, to your days.

I am not happy. I will be open.
I have liked lamps in evening corners, and quiet poems.
There has been fear in my life. Sometimes I speculate
On what a tragedy his life was, really.

Take my hand. Fist my mind in your hand. What are
    you now?
When I was fourteen, I had dreams of suicide,
and I stood at a steep window, at sunset, hoping toward death:
if the light had not melted clouds and plains to beauty,
if light had not transformed that day, I would have leapt.
I am unhappy. I am lonely. Speak to me.

I will be open. I think he never loved me:
he loved the bright beaches, the little lips of foam
that ride small waves, he loved the veer of gulls:
he said with a gay mouth: I love you. Grow to know me.

What are you now? If we could touch one another,
if these our separate entities could come to grips,
clenched like a Chinese puzzle . . . yesterday
I stood in a crowded street that was live with people,
and no one spoke a word, and the morning shone.
Everyone silent, moving . . . Take my hand. Speak to me.

MURIEL RUKEYSER

98 Tea

begonia   When the elephant's-ear in the park
          Shrivelled in frost,
          And the leaves on the paths
          Ran like rats,
          Your lamp-light fell

On shining pillows,
Of sea-shades and sky-shades,
Like umbrellas in Java.

WALLACE STEVENS

99   The Clod and the Pebble

'Love seeketh not itself to please,
Nor for itself hath any care,
But for another gives its ease,
And builds a Heaven in Hell's despair.'

So sung a little Clod of Clay,
Trodden with the cattle's feet,
But a Pebble of the brook
Warbled out these metres meet:

'Love seeketh only self to please,
To bind another to its delight,
Joys in another's loss of ease
And builds a Hell in Heaven's despite.'

WILLIAM BLAKE

100   The Garden of Love

I went to the Garden of Love,
And saw what I never had seen:
A Chapel was built in the midst,
Where I used to play on the green.

And the gates of this Chapel were shut,
And 'Thou shalt not' writ over the door;
So I turn'd to the Garden of Love
That so many sweet flowers bore;

And I saw it was filled with graves,
And tomb-stones where flowers should be;
And priests in black gowns were walking their rounds,
And binding with briars my joys and desires.

WILLIAM BLAKE

101 Home Burial

He saw her from the bottom of the stairs
Before she saw him. She was starting down,
Looking back over her shoulder at some fear.
She took a doubtful step and then undid it
To raise herself and look again. He spoke
Advancing toward her: 'What is it you see
From up there always – for I want to know.'
She turned and sank upon her skirts at that,
And her face changed from terrified to dull.
He said to gain time: 'What is it you see,'
Mounting until she cowered under him.
'I will find out now – you must tell me, dear.'
She, in her place, refused him any help
With the least stiffening of her neck and silence.
She let him look, sure that he wouldn't see,
Blind creature; and awhile he didn't see.
But at last he murmured, 'Oh,' and again, 'Oh.'
'What is it – what?' she said.

                            'Just that I see.'

'You don't,' she challenged. 'Tell me what it is.'

'The wonder is I didn't see at once.
I never noticed it from here before.
I must be wonted to it – that's the reason.
The little graveyard where my people are!
So small the window frames the whole of it.
Not so much larger than a bedroom, is it?
There are three stones of slate and one of marble,
Broad-shouldered little slabs there in the sunlight
On the sidehill. We haven't to mind *those*.
But I understand: it is not the stones,
But the child's mound –'

                            'Don't, don't, don't, don't,' she cried.

She withdrew shrinking from beneath his arm
That rested on the banister, and slid downstairs;
And turned on him with such a daunting look,

He said twice over before he knew himself:
'Can't a man speak of his own child he's lost?'

'Not you! Oh, where's my hat? Oh, I don't need it!
I must get out of here, I must get air.
I don't know rightly whether any man can.'

'Amy! Don't go to someone else this time.
Listen to me. I won't come down the stairs.'
He sat and fixed his chin between his fists.
'There's something I should like to ask you, dear.'

'You don't know how to ask it.'

                    'Help me, then.'

Her fingers moved the latch for all reply.

'My words are nearly always an offence.
I don't know how to speak of anything
So as to please you. But I might be taught
I should suppose. I can't say I see how.
A man must partly give up being a man
With women-folk. We could have some arrangement
By which I'd bind myself to keep hands off
Anything special you're a-mind to name.
Though I don't like such things 'twixt those that love.
Two that don't love can't live together without them.
But two that do can't live together with them.'

She moved the latch a little. 'Don't – don't go.
Don't carry it to someone else this time.
Tell me about it if it's something human.
Let me into your grief. I'm not so much
Unlike other folks as your standing there
Apart would make me out. Give me my chance.
I do think, though, you overdo it a little.
What was it brought you up to think it the thing
To take your mother-loss of a first child
So inconsolably – in the face of love.
You'd think his memory might be satisfied –'

'There you go sneering now!'

'I'm not, I'm not!
You make me angry. I'll come down to you.
God, what a woman! And it's come to this,
A man can't speak of his own child that's dead.'

'You can't because you don't know how to speak.
If you had any feelings, you that dug
With your own hand – how could you? – his little grave;
I saw you from that very window there,
Making the gravel leap and leap in air,
Leap up, like that, like that, and land so lightly
And roll back down the mound beside the hole.
I thought, Who is that man? I didn't know you.
And I crept down the stairs and up the stairs
To look again, and still your spade kept lifting.
Then you came in. I heard your rumbling voice
Out in the kitchen, and I don't know why,
But I went near to see with my own eyes.
You could sit there with the stains on your shoes
Of the fresh earth from your own baby's grave
And talk about your everyday concerns.
You had stood the spade up against the wall
Outside there in the entry, for I saw it.'

'I shall laugh the worst laugh I ever laughed.
I'm cursed. God, if I don't believe I'm cursed.'

'I can repeat the very words you were saying.
"Three foggy mornings and one rainy day
Will rot the best birch fence a man can build."
Think of it, talk like that at such a time!
What had how long it takes a birch to rot
To do with what was in the darkened parlour.
You *couldn't* care! The nearest friends can go
With anyone to death, comes so far short
They might as well not try to go at all.
No, from the time when one is sick to death,
One is alone, and he dies more alone.
Friends make pretence of following to the grave,
But before one is in it, their minds are turned
And making the best of their way back to life

And living people, and things they understand.
But the world's evil. I won't have grief so
If I can change it. Oh, I won't, I won't!'

'There, you have said it all and you feel better.
You won't go now. You're crying. Close the door.
The heart's gone out of it: why keep it up.
Amy! There's someone coming down the road!'

'*You* – oh, you think the talk is all. I must go –
Somewhere out of this house. How can I make you –'

'If – you – do!' She was opening the door wider.
'Where do you mean to go? First tell me that.
I'll follow and bring you back by force. I *will*! –'

ROBERT FROST

102   Death and the Maiden

Once I saw a grown man fall from a tree
and die. That's years ago, I was a girl.
My father's house is sold into a home
for the feeble-minded gentlefolk who can't
any longer stand the world, but in those days
there was money to maintain the mile or so
of discipline that kept the hungry grass
parading to the lake, and once a year
bring men to prune the files of giant trees
whose order satisfied and stood for some
euclidean ancestor's dream about the truth:
elms, most of them, already dying of
their yellow blight, and blackened with witches' broom
in the highest branches – but they could die for years,
decades, so tall their silence, and tell you nothing.
Those men came in October every year,
and among the last leaves, the driven leaves,
would set their ladders for assault and swarm
like pirates into the shrouds, thrusting with hook
and long-handled bill against the withered members
of those great corporations, amputating

death away from the centre. They were called
tree surgeons, on the ground they were surly-
polite and touched their caps, but in the air
they dared. I would watch one straddle a branch
on a day of rainy wind, his red shirt patched
on the elm's great fan of sky, his pruning-claw
breaking the finger-bones from the high hand
which held him, and I'd dream of voyages.
My father said: 'It looks more dangerous
than really it is.' But if your hand offend,
I thought, cut off the hand, and if your eye
offend, pluck out the eye. I looked at him,
out of my window all one afternoon,
and I think he looked back once, a young man
proud and probably lecherous, while I –
was a maiden at a window. Only he died
that day. 'Unlucky boy,' my father said,
who then was dying himself without a word
to anyone, the crab's claw tightening
inside the bowel that year to the next
in dead silence. I do not know if things
that happen can be said to come to pass,
or only happen, but when I remember
my father's house, I imagine sometimes
a dry, ruined spinster at my rainy window
trying to tally on dumb fingers a world's
incredible damage – nothing can stand it! – and
watching the red shirt patched against the sky,
so far and small in the webbed hand of the elm.

HOWARD NEMEROV

103 It's Coming

It's Coming – the postponeless Creature –
It gains the Block – and now – it gains the Door –
Chooses its latch, from all the other fastenings –
Enters – with a 'You know Me – Sir?'

Simple Salute – and Certain Recognition –
Bold – were it Enemy – Brief – were it friend –
Dresses each House in Crape, and Icicle –
And Carries one – out of it – to God –

EMILY DICKINSON

104   There's Been a Death

There's been a Death, in the Opposite House,
As lately as Today –
I know it, by the numb look
Such Houses have – alway –

The Neighbors rustle in and out –
The Doctor – drives away –
A window opens like a Pod –
Abrupt – mechanically –

Somebody flings a Mattress out –
The Children hurry by –
They wonder if it died – on that –
I used to – when a Boy –

The Minister – goes stiffly in –
As if the House were His –
And he owned all the Mourners – now –
And little Boys – besides –

And then the Milliner – and the Man
Of the Appalling Trade –
To take the measure of the House –
There'll be that Dark Parade –

Of Tassels – and of Coaches – soon –
It's easy as a Sign –
The Intuition of the News –
In just a Country Town –

EMILY DICKINSON

105 For Sale

Poor sheepish plaything,
organized with prodigal animosity,
lived in just a year –
my Father's cottage at Beverly Farms
was on the market the month he died.
Empty, open, intimate,
its town-house furniture
had an on tiptoe air
of waiting for the mover
on the heels of the undertaker.
Ready, afraid
of living alone till eighty,
Mother mooned in a window,
as if she had stayed on a train
one stop past her destination.

ROBERT LOWELL

106 Epitaph

This stone was erected, by her fellow-citizens, to the
memory of

ELIZABETH ATKINSON

An industrious woman. She died Jan. the 1st,
1786, aged 77 years.

Periwinks, periwinkle,
    Was ever her cry;
She labour'd to live,
    Poor and honest to die.
At the last day again,
    How her old eyes will twinkle;
For no more will she cry,
    Periwinks, periwinkle!

Ye rich, to virtuous want rejoicing give;
Ye poor, by her example learn to live.

ANONYMOUS

107   Father Dunman's Funeral

'Bury me on a Sunday,'
   He said; 'so as to see
Poor folk there. 'Tis their one day
   To spare for following me.'

With forethought of that Sunday,
   He wrote, while he was well,
On ten rum-bottles one day,
   'Drink for my funeral.'

They buried him on a Sunday,
   That folk should not be balked
His wish, as 'twas their one day:
   And forty couple walked.

They said: 'To have it Sunday
   Was always his concern;
His meaning being that one day
   He'd do us a good turn.

'We must, had it been Monday,
   Have got it over soon,
But now we gain, being Sunday,
   A jolly afternoon.'

THOMAS HARDY

108   Upon his Departure Hence

Thus I
Passe by,
And die:
As One,
Unknown,
And gon:
I'm made
A shade,
And laid
I'th grave,
There have

My Cave.
Where tell
I dwell,
Farewell.

ROBERT HERRICK

109   The Last Mystery

He knew that coastline – no man better –
Knew all its rocks and currents, like the veins
And knuckles on the brown back of his hand;
The leap-frog rollers and tall tons that batter
Boat-rib and man-rib into grains
Of indistinguishable sand:
He had known them all since he could stand.

A shanty was his earliest lullaby,
The beach his back-yard, flotsam all his toys.
He was admitted to the mystery
Of tides; read the wind's writing on the sky;
Could out-sail, out-dive, out-swim boys
Older by half; was known to save
Many from the sabre-toothed, man-eating wave.

Knowing so well the temper of that coast,
And all subaqueous hazards of the sea,
What voice, thought, impulse lugged him from his ale
(When every flag was fighting with a mast
And waves kicked bollards off the quay),
To match his Lilliputian sail
Against the wrestling muscles of the gale?

Only the lemming knows: his friends knew only
Boat-rib and man-rib littered the long shore
Many tides after. I declare he fell
Like a pearl-dazzled diver through the sea
To that last mystery on its floor;
Whose is the heart-beat under the swell,
The hand that turns the whirlpool and the shell?

JON STALLWORTHY

110 Wreaths

1   Each day the tide withdraws; chills us; pastes
The sand with dead gulls, oranges, dead men.
Uttering love, that outlasts or outwastes
Time's attrition, exiles appear again,
But faintly altered in eyes and skin.

2   Into what understanding all have grown!
(Setting aside a few things, the still faces,
Climbing the phosphorous tide, that none will own)
What paradises and watering-places,
What hurts appeased by the sea's handsomeness!

1956

GEOFFREY HILL

111   What Were They Like?

1   Did the people of Viet Nam
    use lanterns of stone?
2   Did they hold ceremonies
    to reverence the opening of buds?
3   Were they inclined to quiet laughter?
4   Did they use bone and ivory,
    jade and silver, for ornament?
5   Had they an epic poem?
6   Did they distinguish between speech and singing?

1 Sir, their light hearts turned to stone.
   It is not remembered whether in gardens
   stone lanterns illumined pleasant ways.
2 Perhaps they gathered once to delight in blossom,
   but after the children were killed
   there were no more buds.
3 Sir, laughter is bitter to the burned mouth.
4 A dream ago, perhaps. Ornament is for joy.
   All the bones were charred.
5 It is not remembered. Remember,
   most were peasants; their life
   was in rice and bamboo.
   When peaceful clouds were reflected in the paddies
   and the water buffalo stepped surely along terraces,
   maybe fathers told their sons old tales.
   When bombs smashed those mirrors
   there was time only to scream.
6 There is an echo yet
   of their speech which was like a song.
   It was reported their singing resembled
   the flight of moths in moonlight.
   Who can say? It is silent now.

DENISE LEVERTOV

112 Nationality

I have grown past hate and bitterness,
I see the world as one;
Yet, though I can no longer hate,
My son is still my son.
   All men at God's round table sit,
   And all men must be fed;
   But this loaf in my hand,
   This loaf is my son's bread.

MARY GILMORE

113 The Latest Decalogue

Thou shalt have one God only; who
Would be at the expense of two?
No graven images may be
Worshipped, except the currency:
Swear not at all; for, for thy curse
Thine enemy is none the worse:
At church on Sunday to attend
Will serve to keep the world thy friend:
Honour thy parents; that is, all
From whom advancement may befall;
Thou shalt not kill; but need'st not strive
Officiously to keep alive:
Do not adultery commit;
Advantage rarely comes of it:
Thou shalt not steal; an empty feat,
When it's so lucrative to cheat:
Bear not false witness; let the lie
Have time on its own wings to fly:
Thou shalt not covet, but tradition
Approves all forms of competition.

ARTHUR HUGH CLOUGH

114 Memories of a Lost War

The guns know what is what, but underneath
In fearful file
We go around burst boots and packs and teeth
That seem to smile.

The scene jags like a strip of celluloid,
A mortar fires,
Cinzano falls, Michelin is destroyed,
The man of tyres.

As darkness drifts like fog in from the sea
Somebody says
'We're digging in.' Look well, for this may be
The last of days.

Hot lightnings stitch the blind eye of the moon,
The thunder's blunt.
We sleep. Our dreams pass in a faint platoon
Toward the front.

Sleep well, for you are young. Each tree and bush
Drips with sweet dew,
And earlier than morning June's cool hush
Will waken you.

The riflemen will wake and hold their breath.
Though they may bleed
They will be proud a while of something death
Still seems to need.

LOUIS SIMPSON

115 The Performance

The last time I saw Donald Armstrong
He was staggering oddly off into the sun,
Going down, of the Philippine Islands.
I let my shovel fall, and put that hand
Above my eyes, and moved some way to one side
That his body might pass through the sun,

And I saw how well he was not
Standing there on his hands,
On his spindle-shanked forearms balanced,
Unbalanced, with his big feet looming and waving
In the great, untrustworthy air
He flew in each night, when it darkened.

Dust fanned in scraped puffs from the earth
Between his arms, and blood turned his face inside out,
To demonstrate its suppleness
Of veins, as he perfected his role.
Next day, he toppled his head off
On an island beach to the south,

And the enemy's two-handed sword
Did not fall from anyone's hands
At that miraculous sight,
As the head rolled over upon
Its wide-eyed face, and fell
Into the inadequate grave

He had dug for himself, under pressure.
Yet I put my flat hand to my eyebrows
Months later, to see him again
In the sun, when I learned how he died,
And imagined him, there,
Come, judged, before his small captors,

Doing all his lean tricks to amaze them –
The back somersault, the kip-up –
And at last, the stand on his hands,
Perfect, with his feet together,
His head down, evenly breathing,
As the sun poured up from the sea

And the headsman broke down
In a blaze of tears, in that light
Of the thin, long human frame
Upside down in its own strange joy,
And, if some other one had not told him,
Would have cut off the feet

Instead of the head,
And if Armstrong had not presently risen
In kingly, round-shouldered attendance,
And then knelt down in himself
Beside his hacked, glittering grave, having done
All things in this life that he could.

JAMES DICKEY

116 The Dying Soldier

'Here are houses,' he moaned,
'I could reach but my brain swims.'
Then they thundered and flashed
And shook the earth to its rims.

'They are gunpits,' he gasped,
'Our men are at the guns.
Water – water – O water
For one of England's dying sons.'

'We cannot give you water
Were all England in your breath.'
'Water – water – O water'
He moaned and swooned to death.

ISAAC ROSENBERG

117 Two Wise Generals

'Not as Black Douglas, bannered, trumpeted,
Who hacked for the casked heart flung to the enemy,
Letting the whole air flow breakneck with blood
Till he fell astride that handful, you and I

Come, two timid and ageing generals
To parley, and to divide the territory
Upon a map, and get honour, and by
This satisfaction part with regiments whole.'

They entered the lit tent, in no hurry to grab.
Apart in darkness twinkled their armies
Like two safe towns. Thus they drank, joked, waxed wise –
So heavily medalled never need fear stab.

The treaty sealed, lands allotted (and a good third
Stuffed down their tunic fronts' private estate)
They left the empty bottle. The tent-lamp out,
They lurched away in the knee-high mist, hearing the first bird,

Towards separate camps.
                Now, one a late dew-moth
Eyes, as he sways, among the still tents. The other roars 'Guard!'
As a fox ducks from the silent parapet. Both
Have found their sleeping armies massacred.

TED HUGHES

118   Before Life and After

A time there was – as one may guess
And as, indeed, earth's testimonies tell –
Before the birth of consciousness,
    When all went well.

None suffered sickness, love, or loss,
None knew regret, starved hope, or heart-burnings;
None cared whatever crash or cross
    Brought wrack to things.

If something ceased, no tongue bewailed,
If something winced and waned, no heart was wrung;
If brightness dimmed, and dark prevailed,
    No sense was stung.

But the disease of feeling germed,
And primal rightness took the tinct of wrong;
Ere nescience shall be reaffirmed
   .How long, how long?

THOMAS HARDY

119 Anthem for Doomed Youth

What passing-bells for these who die as cattle?
    Only the monstrous anger of the guns.
    Only the stuttering rifles' rapid rattle
Can patter out their hasty orisons.
No mockeries for them from prayers or bells,
    Nor any voice of mourning save the choirs, –
The shrill, demented choirs of wailing shells;
    And bugles calling for them from sad shires.

What candles may be held to speed them all?
    Not in the hands of boys, but in their eyes
Shall shine the holy glimmers of good-byes.
    The pallor of girls' brows shall be their pall;
Their flowers the tenderness of silent minds,
And each slow dusk a drawing-down of blinds.

WILFRED OWEN

120 Voices

Bugles sang, saddening the evening air,
And bugles answered, sorrowful to hear.

Voices of boys were by the river-side.
Sleep mothered them; and left the twilight sad.
The shadow of the morrow weighed on men.

Voices of old despondency resigned,
Bowed by the shadow of the morrow, slept.

        dying tone
Of receding voices that will not return.
The wailing of the high far-travelling shells
And the deep cursing of the provoking

The monstrous anger of our taciturn guns.
The majesty of the insults of their mouths.

WILFRED OWEN Unfinished

121 The Next War

War's a joke for me and you,
While we know such dreams are true.
SASSOON

Out there, we've walked quite friendly up to Death;
  Sat down and eaten with him, cool and bland, –
  Pardoned his spilling mess-tins in our hand.
We've sniffed the green thick odour of his breath, –
Our eyes wept, but our courage didn't writhe.
  He's spat at us with bullets and he's coughed
  Shrapnel. We chorused when he sang aloft;
We whistled while he shaved us with his scythe.

Oh, Death was never enemy of ours!
  We laughed at him, we leagued with him, old chum.
No soldier's paid to kick against his powers.
  We laughed, knowing that better men would come,
And greater wars; when each proud fighter brags
He wars on Death – for Life; not men – for flags.

WILFRED OWEN

122 Sonnet

On Seeing a Piece of our Artillery Brought into Action

Be slowly lifted up, thou long black arm,
Great gun towering toward Heaven, about to curse;
Sway steep against them, and for years rehearse
Huge imprecations like a blasting charm!
Reach at that arrogance which needs thy harm,
And beat it down before its sins grow worse;
Spend our resentment, cannon, yea, disburse
Our gold in shapes of flame, our breaths in storm.

Yet, for men's sakes whom thy vast malison
Must wither innocent of enmity,
Be not withdrawn, dark arm, thy spoilure done,
Safe to the bosom of our prosperity.
But when thy spell be cast complete and whole,
May God curse thee, and cut thee from our soul!

WILFRED OWEN

123 Futility

Move him into the sun –
Gently its touch awoke him once,
At home, whispering of fields unsown.
Always it woke him, even in France,
Until this morning and this snow.
If anything might rouse him now
The kind old sun will know.

Think how it wakes the seeds, –
Woke, once, the clays of a cold star.
Are limbs, so dear-achieved, are sides,
Full-nerved – still warm – too hard to stir?
Was it for this the clay grew tall?
– O what made fatuous sunbeams toil
To break earth's sleep at all?

WILFRED OWEN

124 The Parable of the Old Men and the Young

So Abram rose, and clave the wood, and went,
And took the fire with him, and a knife.
And as they sojourned both of them together,
Isaac the first-born spake and said, My Father,
Behold the preparations, fire and iron,
But where the lamb for his burnt-offering?
Then Abram bound the youth with belts and straps,
And builded parapets and trenches there,
And stretched forth the knife to slay his son.
When lo! an angel called him out of heaven,
Saying, Lay not thy hand upon the lad,
Neither do anything to him. Behold,
A ram, caught in a thicket by its horns;
Offer the Ram of Pride instead of him.
But the old man would not so, but slew his son, –
And half the seed of Europe, one by one.

WILFRED OWEN

125 The End

After the blast of lightning from the East,
The flourish of loud clouds, the Chariot Throne;
After the drums of Time have rolled and ceased,
And by the bronze west long retreat is blown,

Shall life renew these bodies? Of a truth
All death will He annul, all tears assuage? –
Fill the void veins of Life again with youth,
And wash, with an immortal water, Age?

When I do ask white Age he saith not so:
'My head hangs weighed with snow.'
And when I hearken to the Earth, she saith:
'My fiery heart shrinks, aching. It is death.
Mine ancient scars shall not be glorified,
Nor my titanic tears, the sea, be dried.'

WILFRED OWEN

126 At a Calvary Near the Ancre

One ever hangs where shelled roads part.
    In this war He too lost a limb,
But His disciples hide apart;
    And now the Soldiers bear with Him.

Near Golgotha strolls many a priest,
    And in their faces there is pride
That they were flesh-marked by the Beast
    By whom the gentle Christ's denied.

The scribes on all the people shove
    And bawl allegiance to the state,
But they who love the greater love
    Lay down their life; they do not hate.

WILFRED OWEN

127 Strange Meeting

It seemed that out of battle I escaped
Down some profound dull tunnel, long since scooped
Through granites which titanic wars had groined.
Yet also there encumbered sleepers groaned,
Too fast in thought or death to be bestirred.
Then, as I probed them, one sprang up, and stared
With piteous recognition in fixed eyes,
Lifting distressful hands as if to bless.
And by his smile, I knew that sullen hall,
By his dead smile I knew we stood in Hell.
With a thousand pains that vision's face was grained;
Yet no blood reached there from the upper ground,
And no guns thumped, or down the flues made moan.
'Strange friend,' I said, 'here is no cause to mourn.'
'None,' said the other, 'save the undone years,
The hopelessness. Whatever hope is yours,
Was my life also; I went hunting wild
After the wildest beauty in the world,
Which lies not calm in eyes, or braided hair,
But mocks the steady running of the hour,
And if it grieves, grieves richlier than here.
For by my glee might many men have laughed,
And of my weeping something had been left,
Which must die now. I mean the truth untold,
The pity of war, the pity war distilled.
Now men will go content with what we spoiled.
Or, discontent, boil bloody, and be spilled.
They will be swift with swiftness of the tigress,
None will break ranks, though nations trek from progress.
Courage was mine, and I had mystery,
Wisdom was mine, and I had mastery;
To miss the march of this retreating world
Into vain citadels that are not walled.
Then, when much blood had clogged their chariot-wheels
I would go up and wash them from sweet wells,
Even with truths that lie too deep for taint.
I would have poured my spirit without stint
But not through wounds; not on the cess of war.

Foreheads of men have bled where no wounds were.
I am the enemy you killed, my friend.
I knew you in this dark; for so you frowned
Yesterday through me as you jabbed and killed.
I parried; but my hands were loath and cold.
Let us sleep now . . .'

WILFRED OWEN

128 Defence

She arrived late, with this motto:
'Time used in reconnaissance
Is not time lost.' Useful hint
On how efficient our defences
Would be. Sent from the Home Office
On 'Work of some importance'.
And 'The first thing' she said
'Is that there will be four minutes
Of preparation before
The thing is dropped. You should
Instruct persons to stand
In the centre of what room
They like – for the blast,
Unlike the bombs of the previous war,
Will draw the walls out.
There will be no crushing
Of flesh. Instead
On all sides walls will reveal
The citizen unharmed.' Here a question,
But 'No' she said 'we have
From our *Intelligence*
Absolute assurance
Our capital is not targeted.'
Total warfare, by arrangement.
And she was sure, when pressed.
'But there will be devastation
As we now suspect, in radius
Of forty-four miles.
The water will be infected;
The light from the thing, astonishing;

Which though surprised by, we should
Not look at; but shelter
Behind some object "to reduce
Damage to the tissue"
From radiation; or shelter
Under brown paper;
Or, if you can, –
Sheets soaked in urine.'

So women who crochet, stop that;
Men labouring whose issue is
The two-handed house, set that aside.
Girls big and delicate
With child, turn on your side;
You will melt. The ravelling spider
And the scorpion whose prongs itch
Will fuse in a viscoid
Tar, black as a huge fly.
The whole of nature
Is a preying upon.
Let man, whose mind is large,
Legislate for
All passionate things,
All sensate things: the sensuous
Grass, whose speech is all
In its sharp, bending blade.
Leave not a leaf, a stone
That rested on the dead
To its own dissolution.

She left then,
As if she were with her feet
Turning an enormous,
If man-made, pearl
As means of locomotion.

JON SILKIN

129 The Enlisted Man

Yelled Corporal Punishment at Private Reasons:
 'Rebels like you have no right to enlist –
 Or to exist!'
Major Considerations leered approval,
 Clenching his fist,
 And gave his fierce moustache a fiercer twist.
So no appeal, even to General Conscience,
 Kept Private Reasons' name off the defaulter-list.

ROBERT GRAVES

130 Our City Is Guarded by Automatic Rockets

1   Breaking every law except the one
    for Go, rolling its porpoise way, the rocket
    staggers on its course; its feelers lock
    a stranglehold ahead; and – rocking – finders
    whispering 'Target, Target', back and forth,
    relocating all its meaning in the dark,
    it freezes on the final stage. I know
    that lift and pour, the flick out of the sky
    and then the power. Power is not enough.

2   Bough touching bough, touching . . . till the shore,
    a lake, an undecided river, and a lake again
    saddling the divide: a world that won't be wise
    and let alone, but instead is found outside
    by little channels, linked by chance, not stern;
    and then when once we're sure we hear a guide
    it fades away toward the opposite end of the road
    from home – the world goes wrong in order to have revenge.
    Our lives are an amnesty given us.

3   There is a place behind our hill so real
    it makes me turn my head, no matter. There
    in the last thicket lies the cornered cat
    saved by its claws, now ready to spend
    all there is left of the wilderness, embracing

its blood. And that is the way that I will spit
life, at the end of any trail where I smell any hunter,
because I think our story should not end –
or go on in the dark with nobody listening.

WILLIAM STAFFORD

131   Domination of Black

At night, by the fire,
The colours of the bushes
And of the fallen leaves,
Repeating themselves,
Turned in the room,
Like the leaves themselves
Turning in the wind.
Yes: but the colour of the heavy hemlocks
Came striding.
And I remembered the cry of the peacocks.

The colours of their tails
Were like the leaves themselves
Turning in the wind,
In the twilight wind.
They swept over the room,
Just as they flew from the boughs of the hemlocks
Down to the ground.
I heard them cry – the peacocks.
Was it a cry against the twilight
Or against the leaves themselves
Turning in the wind,
Turning as the flames
Turned in the fire,
Turning as the tails of the peacocks
Turned in the loud fire,
Loud as the hemlocks
Full of the cry of the peacocks?
Or was it a cry against the hemlocks?

Out of the window,
I saw how the planets gathered
Like the leaves themselves
Turning in the wind.
I saw how the night came,
Came striding like the colour of the heavy hemlocks.
I felt afraid.
And I remembered the cry of the peacocks.

WALLACE STEVENS

132 Death

Nor dread nor hope attend
A dying animal;
A man awaits his end
Dreading and hoping all;
Many times he died,
Many times rose again.
A great man in his pride
Confronting murderous men
Casts derision upon
Supersession of breath;
He knows death to the bone –
Man has created death.

W. B. YEATS

133 Musée des Beaux Arts

About suffering they were never wrong,
The Old Masters: how well they understood
Its human position; how it takes place
While someone else is eating or opening a window or just
   walking dully along;
How, when the aged are reverently, passionately waiting
For the miraculous birth, there always must be
Children who did not specially want it to happen, skating
On a pond at the edge of the wood:
They never forgot
That even the dreadful martyrdom must run its course
Anyhow in a corner, some untidy spot
Where the dogs go on with their doggy life and the torturer's
   horse
Scratches its innocent behind on a tree.

In Brueghel's *Icarus*, for instance: how everything turns away
Quite leisurely from the disaster; the ploughman may
Have heard the splash, the forsaken cry,
But for him it was not an important failure; the sun shone
As it had to on the white legs disappearing into the green
Water; and the expensive delicate ship that must have seen
Something amazing, a boy falling out of the sky,
Had somewhere to get to and sailed calmly on.

W. H. AUDEN

134 Water

If I were called in
To construct a religion
I should make use of water.

Going to church
Would entail a fording
To dry, different clothes;

The litany would employ
Images of sousing,
A furious devout drench,

And I should raise in the east
A glass of water
Where any-angled light
Would congregate endlessly.

PHILIP LARKIN

135 The Twin of Sleep

Death is the twin of Sleep, they say:
    For I shall rise renewed,
Free from the cramps of yesterday,
    Clear-eyed and supple-thewed.

But though this bland analogy
    Helps other folk to face
Decrepitude, senility,
    Madness, disease, disgrace,

I do not like Death's greedy looks:
    Give me his twin instead –
Sleep never auctions off my books,
    My boots, my shirts, my bed.

ROBERT GRAVES

136 Sonnet

O soft embalmer of the still midnight,
Shutting with careful fingers and benign
Our gloom-pleas'd eyes, embower'd from the light,
Enshaded in forgetfulness divine:
O soothest Sleep: if so it please thee, close
In midst of this thine hymn my willing eyes,
Or wait the 'Amen' ere thy poppy throws
Around my bed its lulling charities.
Then save me, or the passèd day will shine
Upon my pillow, breeding many woes,
Save from curious Conscience, that still lords
Its strength for darkness, burrowing like a mole;
Turn the key deftly in the oilèd wards,
And seal the hushed Casket of my Soul.

JOHN KEATS

137 After Long Drought

A tight-lipped hermit, parched of sounds,
That taut sky finally explodes.
Trigger-happy lightning bounds
And flicks the ticklish scalp with goads.

Plumb pregnant clouds in labour's wrack
Floundering, immensely cry
And pour their sputtering pelted pack
Of offspring down the sky.

As if to ape the circus-ring,
Jaws now gape, to gulp apace
Slivering knives of rain that sting
And start each upturned face.

The clap-trap smashed, out rolls a crash
Of rapturous acclaim;
Bright streaming banners stretch, and slash
The air with liquid flame.

JUSTIN ST JOHN

138 A Survey

Down in the Frantic Mountains
they say a canyon winds
crammed with hysterical water
hushed by placid sands.

They tried to map that country,
sent out a field boot crew,
but the river surged at night
and ripped the map in two.

So they sent out wildcats, printed
with intricate lines of fur,
to put their paws with such finesse
the ground was unaware.

Now only the wildcats know it,
patting a tentative paw,
soothing the hackles of ridges,
pouring past rocks and away.

The sun rakes that land each morning;
the mountains buck and scream.
By night the wildcats pad by
gazing it quiet again.

WILLIAM STAFFORD

139 Desert Places

Snow falling and night falling fast, oh, fast
In a field I looked into going past,
And the ground almost covered smooth in snow,
But a few weeds and stubble showing last.

The woods around it have it – it is theirs.
All animals are smothered in their lairs.
I am too absent-spirited to count;
The loneliness includes me unawares.

And lonely as it is that loneliness
Will be more lonely ere it will be less –
A blanker whiteness of benighted snow
With no expression, nothing to express.

They cannot scare me with their empty spaces
Between stars – on stars where no human race is.
I have it in me so much nearer home
To scare myself with my own desert places.

ROBERT FROST

140 Public Bar TV

On a flaked ridge of the desert

Outriders have found foul water. They say nothing;
With the cactus and the petrified tree
Crouch numbed by a wind howling all
Visible horizons equally empty.

The wind brings dust and nothing
Of the wives, the children, the grandmothers
With the ancestral bones, who months ago
Left the last river,

Coming at the pace of oxen.

TED HUGHES

141 Names

A skein of suns, the uncut stones of night,
Calm planets rising, violet, golden, red –
Bear names evolved from man's enormous head:
Of gods who govern battle, rivers, flight,
And goddesses of science and delight;
Arranged in the mortal shapes of those who bled
To found a dynasty or in great dread
Slept with their destiny, full-breasted, white.

But long before stout Venus, clanking Mars,
What appellations had the eternal stars?
When, cheek by jowl with burial pits, rank dens
Lay open to the dark, and dwarfish men
Stared under huge brow-ridges, wits awry,
What fearful monsters slouched about the sky?

ROY FULLER

142 The Trap

The first night that the monster lurched
Out of the forest on all fours,
He saw its shadow in his dream
Circle the house, as though it searched
For one it loved or hated. Claws
On gravel and a rabbit's scream
Ripped the fabric of his dream.

Waking between dark and dawn
And sodden sheets, his reason quelled
The shadow and the nightmare sound.
The second night it crossed the lawn
A brute voice in the darkness yelled.
He struggled up, woke raving, found
His wall-flowers trampled to the ground.

When rook wings beckoned the shadows back
He took his rifle down, and stood
All night against the leaded glass.
The moon ticked round. He saw the black
Elm-skeletons in the doomsday wood,
The sailing and the failing stars
And red coals dropping between bars.

The third night such a putrid breath
Fouled, flared his nostrils, that he turned,
Turned, but could not lift, his head.
A coverlet as thick as death
Oppressed him: he crawled out: discerned
Across the door his watchdog, dead.
'Build a trap,' the neighbours said.

All that day he built his trap
With metal jaws and a spring as thick
As the neck of a man. One touch
Triggered the hanging teeth : jump, snap,
And lightning guillotined the stick
Thrust in its throat. With gun and torch
He set his engine in the porch.

The fourth night in their beds appalled
His neighbours heard the hunting roar
Mount, mount to an exultant shriek.
At daybreak timidly they called
His name, climbed through the splintered door,
And found him sprawling in the wreck,
Naked, with a severed neck.

JON STALLWORTHY

143 Hurt Hawks

The broken pillar of the wing jags from the clotted shoulder,
The wing trails like a banner in defeat,
No more to use the sky forever but live with famine
And pain a few days : cat nor coyote
Will shorten the week of waiting for death, there is game
    without talons.
He stands under the oak-bush and waits
The lame feet of salvation ; at night he remembers freedom
And flies in a dream, the dawns ruin it.
He is strong and pain is worse to the strong, incapacity is
    worse.
The curs of the day come and torment him
At distance, no one but death the redeemer will humble that
    head,
The intrepid readiness, the terrible eyes.
The wild God of the world is sometimes merciful to those
That ask mercy, not often to the arrogant.
You do not know him, you communal people, or you have
    forgotten him ;
Intemperate and savage, the hawk remembers him ;
Beautiful and wild, the hawks, and men that are dying,
    remember him.

I'd sooner, except the penalties, kill a man than a hawk; but
the great redtail
Had nothing left but unable misery
From the bone too shattered for mending, the wing that trailed
under his talons when he moved.
We had fed him six weeks, I gave him freedom,
He wandered over the foreland hill and returned in the
evening, asking for death,
Not like a beggar, still eyed with the old
Implacable arrogance. I gave him the lead gift in the twilight.
What fell was relaxed,
Owl-downy, soft feminine feathers; but what
Soared: the fierce rush: the night-herons by the flooded river
cried for fear at its rising
Before it was quite unsheathed from reality.

ROBINSON JEFFERS

144 All-In Wrestlers

These two great men battling like lovers
Groan and pant in limbs that strangle,
Hold and abandon, clip and part.
Such is their longing for one another.
Each is the other's bitter angel,
Yet for love they wrestle, heart to heart.

They stand as close together
As those two young workmen, one of whom
Removes with the wetted corner of
His crumpled handkerchief a splinter
From his mate's left eye, a dumb
Show of man's concern for man, a silent love.

But then a leg is hooked, an arm once more
Is pressed beyond the limits of desire,
And one upon the other falls, who with a yell
Full of imploring anger beats the floor
With helpless fist, while his enemy, with cruel fire,
Grapples the loser to his breast, and screws him into hell.

JAMES KIRKUP

145 Cat-Faith

As a cat, caught by the door opening,
on the perilous top shelf, red-jawed and raspberry-clawed,
lets itself fall floorward without looking,
sure by cat-instinct it will find the ground
where innocence is; and falls
anyhow, in a furball, so fast that the eye
misses the twist and trust
that come from having fallen before,
and only notices cat silking away,
crime inconceivable in so meek a walk,

so do we let ourselves fall morningward
through shelves of dream. When, libertine at dark,
we let the visions in, and the black window
grotesques us back, our world unbalances.
Many-faced monsters of our own devising
jostle at the verge of sleep, as the room
loses its edges and grows hazed and haunted
by words murmured or by woes remembered,
till, sleep-dissolved, we fall, the known world leaves us,
and room and dream and self and safety melt
into a final madness, where any landscape
may easily curdle, and the dead cry out . . .

but ultimately, it ebbs. Voices recede.
The pale square of the window glows and stays.
Slowly the room arrives and dawns, and we
arrive in our selves. Last night, last week, the past
leak back, awake. As light solidifies,
dream dims. Outside, the washed hush of the garden
waits patiently, and, newcomers from death,
how gratefully we draw its breath!
Yet, to endure that unknown night by night,
must we not be sure, with cat-insight,
we can afford its terrors, and that full day
will find us at the desk, sane, unafraid –
cheeks shaven, letters written, bills paid?

ALASTAIR REID

146 Birds

Whatever the bird is, is perfect in the bird.
Weapon kestrel hard as a blade's curve,
thrush round as a mother or a full drop of water,
fruit-green parrot wise in his shrieking swerve –
all are what bird is and do not reach beyond bird.

Whatever the bird does is right for the bird to do –
cruel kestrel dividing in his hunger the sky,
thrush in the trembling dew beginning to sing,
parrot clinging and quarrelling and veiling his queer eye –
all these are as birds are and good for birds to do.

But I am torn and beleaguered by my own people.
The blood that feeds my heart is the blood they gave me,
and my heart is the house where they gather and fight for
    dominion –
all different, all with a wish and a will to save me,
to turn me into the ways of other people.

If I could leave their battleground for the forest of a bird
I could melt the past, the present and the future in one
and find the words that lie behind all these languages.
Then I could fuse my passions into one clear stone
and be simple to myself as the bird is to the bird.

JUDITH WRIGHT

147 The Red Cockatoo

Sent as a present from Annam –
A red cockatoo.
Coloured like the peach-tree blossom,
Speaking with the speech of men.
And they did to it what is always done
To the learned and eloquent.
They took a cage with stout bars
And shut it up inside.

ANONYMOUS Translated from the Chinese by Arthur Waley

148 God's Grandeur

The world is charged with the grandeur of God.
  It will flame out, like shining from shook foil;
  It gathers to a greatness, like the ooze of oil
Crushed. Why do men then now not reck his rod?
Generations have trod, have trod, have trod;
  And all is seared with trade; bleared, smeared with toil;
  And wears man's smudge and shares man's smell: the soil
Is bare now, nor can foot feel, being shod.

And for all this, nature is never spent;
  There lives the dearest freshness deep down things;
And though the last lights off the black West went
  Oh, morning, at the brown brink eastward, springs –
Because the Holy Ghost over the bent
  World broods with warm breast and with ah! bright wings.

GERARD MANLEY HOPKINS

149 Pigeons

On the crooked arm of Columbus, on his cloak,
they mimic his blind and statuary stare,
and the chipped profiles of his handmaidens
they adorn with droppings. Over the loud square,
from all the arms and ledges of their rest,
only a bread crust or a bell unshelves them.
Adding to Atlas' globe, they dispose themselves
with a fat propriety, and pose as garlands
importantly about his burdened shoulders.
Occasionally a lift of wind uncarves them.

   Stone becomes them; they, in their turn, become it.
Their opal eyes have a monumental cast.
And, in a maze of noise,
their quiet *croomb croomb* dignifies the spaces,
suggesting the sound of silence. On cobbled islands,
marooned in tantrums of traffic, they know their place,
faithful and anonymous, like servants,
and never beg, but properly receive.

   Arriving in rainbows of oil-and-water feathers,
they fountain down from buttresses and outcrops,
from Fontainebleau and London,
and, squat on the margins of roofs, with a gargoyle look,
they note, from an edge of air, with hooded eyes,
the city slowly lessening the sky.

   All praise to them who nightly in the parks
keep peace for us; who, cosmopolitan,
patrol and people all cathedraled places,
and easily, lazily haunt and inhabit
St Paul's, St Peter's, or the Madeleine,
the paved courts of the past, pompous as keepers
a sober race of messengers and custodians,
neat in their international uniforms,
alighting with a word perhaps from Rome.
Permanence is their business, space and time
their special preservations; and wherever
the great stone men we save from death are stationed,
appropriately on the head of each is perched,
as though for ever, his appointed pigeon.

ALASTAIR REID

150　Wedgebury Cocking

At Wedgebury there was a cocking,
A match between Newton and Scroggins.
The colliers and nailers left work,
And all to old Spittle's went jogging.

　Ri-fol-diddy, Rol-diddy, Fol-diddy, Rol-diddy,
　Rol-diddy, Rol-diddy, ay yoh.

To see this noble sport
Many noble men resorted,
And though they'd little of money
With that they freely sported.

There was Jeffory and Oldborn from 'ampton
And Dusty from Bilston was there,
Plummery he came from Darlaston
And he was rude as a bear.

Old Will he come from Walsall,
And Smacker from West Brom' come,
Blind Robin he came from Rowley,
And staggering he went wum.

home

Rough Moey come hobbling along
As though he some cripple was mocking,
To join in the blackguard throng
That met at Wedgebury Cocking.

He borrowed a trifle of Doll
To back old Taverner's grey,
He laid fourpence halfpenny to fourpence,
Then lost and went broken away.

But soon he returned to the pit,
For he'd borrowed a trifle of money,
And ventured another large bet,
Along with blobber-mouth Coney.

When Coney demanded his money,
Which is common on all such occasions,
He cried, 'Blast thee! If thee doesn't hold thy peace,
I'll pay thee as Paul paid the 'phesians.'

Scroggins' breeches were made of nankeen,
And wore very thin in the groin:
In stooping to handle his cock
His buttocks burst out behind.

The morning's sport being over
Old Spittle a dinner proclaimed;
Each man he should dine for a groat;
If he grumbled he ought to be damned,

For there was plenty of beef;
But Spittle he swore by his troth
That never a man should dine
Till he'd eaten his noggin of broth.

Bunny Hyde got a lump in his throat
As was like to have stopped his breath;
The beef it was old and tough,
Off a bull that was baited to death.

The company all fell in confusion
At seeing poor Bunny Hyde choke,
They took him into the kitchen
And held his head over the smoke.

They held him so close to the fire
He frizzled just like a beef steak
Then threw him down on the floor
Which had like to have broken his neck.

One gi'd him a kick of the stomach
Another a poke of the brow;
His wife said, 'Throw him in the stable;
And he'll be better just now.'

Then they all returned to the pit
And the fighting went forward again
Six battles were fought on each side,
And the next to decide the main,

For they were two famous cocks
As ever this country bred,
Scroggins' a duck-winged black,
And Newton's a shift-wing red.

The conflict was hard on both sides,
Till Brassy's duck-winged was choked
The colliers were tarnationly vexed,
And the nailers were sorely provoked.

Peter Stephens he swore a great oath
That Scroggins had played his cock foul;
Scroggins he gave him a kick
And cried, 'God damn thy soul.'

The company then fell in discord,
A bloody fight did ensue;
Kick, bludgeon and bite was the word,
Till the Walsall men were subdued.

Rough Moey bit off a man's nose,
And wished that he could have him slain,
So they trampled both cocks to death
And they made a draw of the main.

The cock-pit was near to the church,
An ornament unto the town,
On one side was an old coal-pit,
The other well gorsed around.

Peter Hadley peeped through the gorse
On purpose to see the cocks fight;
Spittle bodged his eye out with a fork
And said, 'Damn thee, that serves thee right.'

Some people may think this is strange
Who Wedgebury never knew,
But those who have ever been there
Won't have the least doubt but it's true.

For they are savage by nature
And guilty of deeds most shocking;
Jack Baker he wacked his own father
And so ended Wedgebury Cocking.

TRADITIONAL

151　Thirteen Ways of Looking at a Blackbird

1　Among twenty snowy mountains,
The only moving thing
Was the eye of the blackbird.

2　I was of three minds,
Like a tree
In which there are three blackbirds.

3　The blackbird whirled in the autumn winds.
It was a small part of the pantomime.

4　A man and a woman
Are one.
A man and a woman and a blackbird.
Are one.

5　I do not know which to prefer,
The beauty of inflections
Or the beauty of innuendoes,
The blackbird whistling
Or just after.

6　Icicles filled the long window
With barbaric glass.
The shadow of the blackbird
Crossed it, to and fro.
The mood
Traced in the shadow
An indecipherable cause.

7　O thin men of Haddam,
Why do you imagine golden birds?
Do you not see how the blackbird
Walks around the feet
Of the women about you?

8　I know noble accents
And lucid, inescapable rhythms;
But I know, too,
That the blackbird is involved
In what I know.

9   When the blackbird flew out of sight,
It marked the edge
Of one of many circles.

10   At the sight of blackbirds
Flying in a green light,
Even the bawds of euphony
Would cry out sharply.

11   He rode over Connecticut
In a glass coach.
Once, a fear pierced him,
In that he mistook
The shadow of his equipage
For blackbirds.

12   The river is moving.
The blackbird must be flying.

13   It was evening all afternoon.
It was snowing
And it was going to snow.
The blackbird sat
In the cedar-limbs.

WALLACE STEVENS

152 Blue Umbrellas

'The thing that makes a blue umbrella with its tail –
How do you call it?' you ask. Poorly and pale
Comes my answer. For all I can call it is peacock.

Now that you go to school, you will learn how we call all sorts
    of things;
How we mar great works by our mean recital.
You will learn, for instance, that Head Monster is not the
    gentleman's accepted title;
The blue-tailed eccentrics will be merely peacocks; the dead
    bird will no longer doze
Off till tomorrow's lark, for the letter has killed him.
The dictionary is opening, the gay umbrellas close.

Oh our mistaken teachers ! –
It was not a proper respect for words that we need,
But a decent regard for things, those older creatures and more
real.
Later you may even resort to writing verse
To prove the dishonesty of names and their black greed –
To confess your ignorance, to expiate your crime, seeking one
spell to lift another curse.
Or you may, more commodiously, spy on your children, busy
discoverers,
Without the dubious benefit of rhyme.

D. J. ENRIGHT

153 Snow

In the gloom of whiteness,
In the great silence of snow,
A child was sighing
And bitterly saying : 'Oh,
They have killed a white bird up there on her nest,
The down is fluttering from her breast !'
And still it fell through that dusky brightness
On the child crying for the bird of the snow.

EDWARD THOMAS

154 The Snow Fences

They are fencing the upland against
the drifts this wind, those clouds
would bury it under : brow and bone
know already that levelling zero
as you go, an aching skeleton,
in the breathtaking rareness of winter air.

Walking here, what do you see ?
Little more, through wind-teased eyes,
than a black, iron tree
and, there, another, a straggle

of low and broken wall between, grass
sapped of its greenness, day going.

The farms are few : spread
as wide, perhaps, as when
the Saxons who found them, chose
these airy and woodless spaces
and froze here before they fed
the unsuperseded burial ground.

Ahead, the church's dead-white
limewash will dazzle the mind
as, dazed, you enter to escape :
despite the stillness here, the chill
of wash-light scarcely seems
less penetrant than the hill-top wind.

Between the graves, you find
a beheaded pigeon, the blood and grain
trailed from its bitten crop, as alien to all
the day's pallor as the raw
wounds of the earth, turned above
a fresh solitary burial.

A plaque of staining metal
distinguishes this grave among
an anonymity whose stones
the frosts have scaled, thrusting under
as if they grudged the ground
its ill-kept memorials.

The bitter darkness drives you
back valleywards, and again you bend
joint and tendon to encounter
the wind's force and leave behind
the nameless stones, the snow-shrouds
of a waste season : they are fencing
the upland against those years, those clouds.

CHARLES TOMLINSON

155 It Sifts from Leaden Sieves

It sifts from Leaden Sieves –
It powders all the Wood.
It fills with Alabaster Wool
The Wrinkles of the Road –

It makes an Even Face
Of Mountain, and of Plain –
Unbroken Forehead from the East
Unto the East again –

It reaches to the Fence –
It wraps it Rail by Rail
Till it is lost in Fleeces –
It deals Celestial Vail

To Stump, and Stack – and Stem –
A Summer's empty Room ! –
Acres of Joints, where Harvests were,
Recordless, but for them –

It Ruffles Wrists of Posts
As Ankles of a Queen –
Then stills its Artisans – like Ghosts –
Denying they have been –

EMILY DICKINSON

156 The Snow Man

One must have a mind of winter
To regard the frost and the boughs
Of the pine-trees crusted with snow ;

And have been cold a long time
To behold the junipers shagged with ice,
The spruces rough in the distant glitter

Of the January sun ; and not to think
Of any misery in the sound of the wind,
In the sound of a few leaves,

Which is the sound of the land
Full of the same wind
That is blowing in the same bare place

For the listener, who listens in the snow,
And, nothing himself, beholds
Nothing that is not there and the nothing that is.

WALLACE STEVENS

157 Sayings from the Northern Ice

It is people at the edge who say
things at the edge: winter is toward knowing.

> Sled runners before they meet have long talk apart.
> There is a pup in every litter the wolves will have.
> A knife that falls points at an enemy.
> Rocks in the wind know their place: down low.
> Over your shoulder is God; the dying deer sees him.

At the mouth of the long sack we fall in forever
storms brighten the spikes of the stars.

> Wind that buried bear skulls north of here
> and beats moth wings for help outside the door
> is bringing bear skull wisdom, but do not ask the skull
> too large a question till summer.
> Something too dark was held in that strong bone.

Better to end with a lucky saying:

> Sled runners cannot decide to join or to part.
> When they decide, it is a bad day.

WILLIAM STAFFORD

158 Ice-Fishing

Not thinking other than how the hand works
I wait until dark here on the cold
world rind, ice-curved over simplest rock
where the tugged river flows over hidden
springs too insidious to be quite forgotten.

When the night comes I plunge my hand
where the string of fish know their share
of the minimum. Then, bringing back my hand
is a great sunburst event; and slow
home with me over unmarked snow

In the wild flipping warmth of won-back thought
my boots, my hat, my body go.

WILLIAM STAFFORD

159 Juggler

A ball will bounce, but less and less. It's not
A light-hearted thing, resents its own resilience.
Falling is what it loves, and the earth falls
So in our hearts from brilliance,
Settles and is forgot.
It takes a sky-blue juggler with five red balls

To shake our gravity up. Whee, in the air
The balls roll round, wheel on his wheeling hands,
Learning the ways of lightness, alter to spheres
Grazing his finger ends,
Cling to their courses there,
Swinging a small heaven about his ears.

But a heaven is easier made of nothing at all
Than the earth regained, and still and sole within
The spin of worlds, with a gesture sure and noble
He reels that heaven in,
Landing it ball by ball,
And trades it all for a broom, a plate, a table.

Oh, on his toe the table is turning, the broom's
Balancing up on his nose, and the plate whirls
On the tip of the broom! Damn, what a show, we cry:
The boys stamp, and the girls
Shriek, and the drum booms
And all comes down, and he bows and says good-bye.

If the juggler is tired now, if the broom stands
In the dust again, if the table starts to drop
Through the daily dark again, and though the plate
Lies flat on the table top,
For him we batter our hands
Who has won for once over the world's weight.

RICHARD WILBUR

160 Hazardous Occupations

Jugglers keep six bottles in the air.
Club swingers toss up six and eight.
The knife throwers miss each other's
        ears by a hair and the steel quivers
        in the target wood.
The trapeze battlers do a back-and-forth
        high in the air with a girl's feet
        and ankles upside down.
So they earn a living – till they miss
        once, twice, even three times.
So they live on hate and love as gypsies
        live in satin skins and shiny eyes.
In their graves do the elbows jostle once
        in a blue moon – and wriggle to throw
        a kiss answering a dreamed-of applause?
Do the bones repeat: It's a good act –
        we got a good hand . . . ?

CARL SANDBURG

161 The Midnight Skaters

The hop-poles stand in cones,
　　The icy pond lurks under,
The pole-tops steeple to the thrones
　　Of stars, sound gulfs of wonder;
But not the tallest there, 'tis said,
Could fathom to the pond's black bed.

Then is not death at watch
　　Within those secret waters?
What wants he but to catch
　　Earth's heedless sons and daughters?
With but a crystal parapet
Between, he has his engines set.

Then on, blood shouts, on, on,
　　Twirl, wheel and whip above him,
Dance on this ball-floor thin and wan,
　　Use him as though you love him;
Court him, elude him, reel and pass,
And let him hate you through the glass.

EDMUND BLUNDEN

162 An Empty Threat

I stay;
But it isn't as if
There wasn't always Hudson's Bay
And the fur trade,
A small skiff
And a paddle blade.

I can just see my tent pegged,
And me on the floor,
Crosslegged,
And a trapper looking in at the door
With furs to sell.

His name's Joe,
Alias John,
And between what he doesn't know
And won't tell
About where Henry Hudson's gone,
I can't say he's much help;
But we get on.

The sea yelp
On an ice cake.
It's not men by some mistake?

No,
There's not a soul
For a wind-break
Between me and the North Pole –

Except always John-Joe,
My French Indian Esquimaux,
And he's off setting traps,
In one himself perhaps.

Give a head shake
Over so much bay
Thrown away
In snow and mist
That doesn't exist,
I was going to say,
For God, man or beast's sake,
Yet does perhaps for all three.

Don't ask Joe
What it is to him.
It's sometimes dim
What it is to me,
Unless it be
It's the old captain's dark fate
Who failed to find or force a strait
In its two-thousand-mile coast;
And his crew left him where he failed,
And nothing came of all he sailed.

It's to say, 'You and I'
To such a ghost,
'You and I
Off here
With the dead race of the Great Auk!'
And, 'Better defeat almost,
If seen clear,
Than life's victories of doubt
That need endless talk talk
To make them out.'

ROBERT FROST

163 Vacation

One scene as I bow to pour her coffee: –

Three Indians in the scouring drouth
huddle at a grave scooped in the gravel,
lean to the wind as our train goes by.
Someone is gone.
There is dust on everything in Nevada.

I pour the cream.

WILLIAM STAFFORD

164 A January Night

The rain smites more and more,
The east wind snarls and sneezes;
Through the joints of the quivering door
    The water wheezes.

The tip of each ivy-shoot
Writhes on its neighbour's face;
There is some hid dread afoot
    That we cannot trace.

Is it the spirit astray
Of the man at the house below
Whose coffin they took in today?
    We do not know.

THOMAS HARDY

165 At Day-Close in November

The ten hours' light is abating,
  And a late bird wings across,
Where the pines, like waltzers waiting,
  Give their black heads a toss.

Beech leaves, that yellow the noon-time,
  Float past like specks in the eye;
I set every tree in my June time,
  And now they obscure the sky.

And the children who ramble through here
  Conceive that there never has been
A time when no tall trees grew here,
  That none will in time be seen.

THOMAS HARDY

166 Patterns of Earth

Now the new grass is vivid with dandelions,
As last night the ancient sky was constellated.

And the Scorpion, the Dog, Perseus, and Hercules
Are less than the gold children of my field.

Whom I will name quickly for their time is flying:
The Butcher, the Baker, and the Candlestick maker.

They will be gone in a fortnight, full upon the wind
And the bullies of the sky will resume their mastery.

HYAM PLUTZIK

167 A Boy's Head

In it there is a space-ship
and a project
for doing away with piano lessons.

And there is
Noah's ark,
which shall be first.

And there is
an entirely new bird,
an entirely new hare,
an entirely new bumble-bee.

There is a river
that flows upwards.

There is a multiplication table.

There is anti-matter.

And it just cannot be trimmed.

I believe
that only what cannot be trimmed
is a head.

There is much promise
in the circumstance
that so many people have heads.

MIROSLAV HOLUB Translated from the Czech by Ian Milner

168 Wanting the Impossible

Suppose he wishes balloon routes
        to five new moons, one woman,
        and a two-acre bean farm with
        bean poles and waltzing scare-
        crows wearing clown hats:
Ah-hah, ah-hah, this to God,
        this to me, this is something.

CARL SANDBURG

169 How to Paint a Perfect Christmas

Above, you paint the sky
delicate as maidenhair.
Below, pour a little darkness
heated to room temperature
or slightly more.

With a cat's claw in the dark
scratch out a little tree,
the finest tree in the world,
finer than any forester
could ever imagine.

And the tree itself
will light up
and the whole picture purr
with green joy,
with purple hope.

Right. But now you must
put under the tree
the
real big thing,
the thing you most want in the world;
the thing pop-singers
call happiness.

It's easy enough for a cat,
a cat will put a mouse there,
Colonel Blimp will line up
the largest jet-propelled halberd
which shoots and bangs and salutes,
a sparrow will gather
a few stalks for its nest,
mister junior clerk will submit
a stuffed file tied with red tape,
a butterfly will put there
a new rubber peacock's eye,
but what will *you* put there?

You think and think
till the day grows grey,
till the river almost runs out,
till even the bulbs begin to yawn,
you think

and finally

there in the darkness you blot out
a hazy white spot,
a bit like a florin,
a bit like a ship,
a bit like a Moon,
a bit like the beautiful face
of someone (who?) else,

a hazy white spot,
perhaps more like emptiness,
like the negation of something,
like non-pain,
like non-fear,
like non-worry,

a hazy white spot,
and you go to bed
and say to yourself,
yes, now I know how to do it,
yes, now I know,
yes,
next time
I shall paint
the most perfect Christmas
that ever was.

MIROSLAV HOLUB Translated from the Czech by Ian Milner and George Theiner

170 Wings

We have
a microscopic anatomy
of the whale
this
gives
Man
assurance
WILLIAM CARLOS WILLIAMS

We have
a map of the universe
for microbes,
we have
a map of a microbe
for the universe.

We have
a Grand Master of chess
made of electronic circuits.

But above all
we have
the ability
to sort peas,
to cup water in our hands,
to seek
the right screw
under the sofa
for hours.

This
gives us
wings.

MIROSLAV HOLUB Translated from the Czech by George Theiner

171 Felix Randal

blacksmith

Felix Randal the farrier, O he is dead then? my duty all ended,
Who have watched his mould of man, big-boned and hardy-
    handsome
Pining, pining, till time when reason rambled in it and some
Fatal four disorders, fleshed there, all contended?

Sickness broke him. Impatient, he cursed at first, but mended
Being anointed and all; though a heavenlier heart began some
Months earlier, since I had our sweet reprieve and ransom
Tendered to him. Ah well, God rest him all road ever he
    offended!

makes of
greater worth

This seeing the sick endears them to us, us too it endears.
My tongue had taught thee comfort, touch had quenched thy
    tears,
Thy tears that touched my heart, child, Felix, poor Felix
    Randal;

How far from then forethought of, all thy more boisterous
    years,
When thou at the random grim forge, powerful amidst peers,

prepare

Didst fettle for the great grey drayhorse his bright and battering
    sandal!

GERARD MANLEY HOPKINS

172 Thistles

Against the rubber tongues of cows and the hoeing hands of
    men
Thistles spike the summer air
Or crackle open under a blue-black pressure.

Every one a revengeful burst
Of resurrection, a grasped fistful
Of splintered weapons and Icelandic frost thrust up

From the underground stain of a decayed Viking.
They are like pale hair and the gutturals of dialects.
Every one manages a plume of blood.

Then they grow grey, like men.
Mown down, it is a feud. Their sons appear,
Stiff with weapons, fighting back over the same ground.

TED HUGHES

173 As Sure as What is Most Sure

from *St Winefred's Well*

As sure as what is most sure, sure as that spring primroses
Shall new-dapple next year, sure as tomorrow morning,
Amongst come-back-again things, things with a revival,
    things with a recovery.

GERARD MANLEY HOPKINS

174 Lament

Because I have no time
To set my ladder up, and climb
Out of the dung and straw,
Green poems laid in a dark store
Shrivel and grow soft
Like unturned apples in a loft.

JON STALLWORTHY

175 The Secret

Two girls discover
the secret of life
in a sudden line of
poetry.

I who don't know the
secret wrote
the line. They
told me

(through a third person)
they had found it
but not what it was,
not even

what line it was. No doubt
by now, more than a week
later, they have forgotten
the secret,

the line, the name of
the poem. I love them
for finding what
I can't find,

and for loving me
for the line I wrote,
and for forgetting it
so that

a thousand times, till death
finds them, they may
discover it again, in other
lines,

in other
happenings. And for
wanting to know it,
for

assuming there is
such a secret, yes,
for that
most of all.

DENISE LEVERTOV

176 Snatch of Sliphorn Jazz

Are you happy? It's the only
way to be, kid.
Yes, be happy, it's a good nice
way to be.
But not happy-happy, kid, don't
be too doubled-up doggone happy.
It's the doubled-up doggone happy-
happy people . . . bust hard . . . they
do bust hard . . . when they bust.
Be happy, kid, go to it, but not too
doggone happy.

CARL SANDBURG

177 Useless

The after-thought
Is good for nought –
Except it be
To catch blind horses wi'.

TRADITIONAL

178 F for Francis

F for Francis,
I for Jancis,
N for Nickley Boney,
I for John the Waterman, and
S for Signey Coney.

TRADITIONAL

Tunes for Some Poems

46 Sair Fyeld, Hinny

Sair fyeld—, hinny, sair fyeld— now—,
Sair fyeld—, hinny, sin' I ken – ned thou.
I was young and lus - ty—, I was fair and clear
I was young and lus - ty—, man - ya long—
year. Sair fyeld, hinny—, sair fyeld— now—,
Sair fyeld—, hinny, sin' I ken – ned thou.

72 The Unquiet Grave

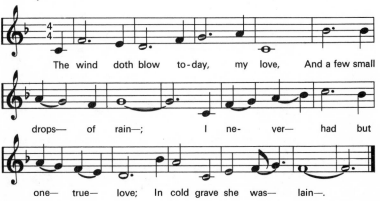

The wind doth blow to - day, my love, And a few small
drops— of rain—; I ne - ver— had but
one— true— love; In cold grave she was— lain—.

76 Ballad

A faith-less shep-herd— court-ed me, He
stole a-way my li- ber-ty; When my poor heart was
strange— to men He came and smiled and stole it— then.

85 The Royal Duke of Grantham

Six dukes went a- fish- ing Down by— yon seaside. One of them spied a dead bo-dy Come
float-ing on the tide.

86 She's like the Swallow

She's like the swal-low that flies so high, She's
like the ri-ver that never runs dry, She's like the sun- shine
on the lee shore, I love my love— and love is no more.

150 Wedgebury Cocking

At Wedge-bu-ry there was a cock-ing, A— match between New-ton and Scrog-gins. The col-liers and nail-ers
left work, And— all to old Spitt-le's went jog-ging.
Ri - fol-did-dy, Rol-did-dy, Fol-did-dy, Rol-did-dy
Rol- did- dy, Rol- did- dy, ay yoh.

Acknowledgements

For permission to use copyright material acknowledgement is made to the following:

Poems For 50 and 132 to W. H. Auden and Faber and Faber Ltd; for 161 to Edmund Blunden; for 8 to Ronald Bottrall; for 35 to The Swallow Press Inc.; for the translations of 79 and 80 to Penguin Books Ltd; for 55 from *Modern Folk Ballads* by Charles Causley to Charles Causley, Studio Vista Ltd and David Higham Associates Ltd; for 90 from *Union Street* by Charles Causley to Charles Causley, Rupert Hart-Davis Ltd and David Higham Associates Ltd; for 21, 76 and 83 to Eric Robinson; for 78 and 82 from *The Spice-Box of Earth* by Leonard Cohen to McClelland and Stewart Ltd, Toronto; for 43 from *With Love Somehow* by Tony Connor to the Oxford University Press; for 57 and 93 from *Poems 1950–65* by Robert Creeley to Calder and Boyars Ltd; for 22 by Roland Tombekai Dempster from *Poems from Black Africa* to Indiana University Press; for 115 to Calder and Boyars Ltd; for 103, 104 and 155 from Thomas H. Johnson (ed.), *the Poems of Emily Dickinson*, to the President and Fellows of Harvard College and Harvard University Press; for 12 and 40 to William Empson and Chatto and Windus Ltd; for 152 from *Bread Rather than Blossoms* by D. J. Enright to Martin Secker and Warburg Ltd; for the translation of 10 to Arthur Barker Ltd; for 96, 101, 139 and 162 from *The Complete Poems of Robert Frost* to Jonathan Cape Ltd, Holt Rinehart and Winston Inc. and Laurence Pollinger Ltd; for 77 and 94 from *Enter Without Knocking* by Dennis Glover to the Pegasus Press Ltd; for 39, 81, 95, 129. and 135 from *Collected Poems 1965* by Robert Graves to Robert Graves; for 54 to Faber and Faber Ltd; for 73, 107, 118, 164 and 165 from *The Collected Poems of Thomas Hardy* to the Trustees of the Hardy Estate, The Macmillan Company of Canada and Macmillan and Co. Ltd; for 13 to Faber and Faber Ltd; for 110 to Geoffrey Hill and Andre Deutsch Ltd; for 167, 169 and 170 to Penguin Books Ltd; for 23, 59, 148, 171 and 173 from *Collected Works of Gerard Manley Hopkins* to the Oxford University Press; for 117, 140 and 172 to Faber and Faber Ltd; for 2 from *The Lost World* by Randell Jarrell to Eyre and Spottiswoode Ltd; for 143 to Random House Inc.; for 144 to James Kirkup; for 3 and 134 to Faber and Faber Ltd; for 36, 37, 45, 47 and 52 to Laurence Pollinger Ltd and the Estate of the late Mrs Frieda Lawrence; for 1 and 175 from *O Taste and See* by Denise Levertov to New Directions Publishing Corporation; for 26 from *The Jacob's Ladder* and 111 from *The Sorrow Dance* by Denise Levertov to Jonathan Cape Ltd, New Directions Publishing Corporation and Laurence Pollinger Ltd; for 65 to the University of Chicago Press; for 105 to Faber and Faber Ltd; for 7 and 51 from *Surroundings* and 25 from *Riding Lights* by Norman MacCaig to Norman MacCaig and Chatto and Windus Ltd; for 53 to The Caxton Press; for 41 to Penguin Books Ltd; for 64 from *Scottish Poetry Number One* to the Edinburgh University Press; for 102 by Howard Nemerov from *Five American Poets* to Faber and Faber Ltd and Laurence Pollinger Ltd; for 119, 120, 121, 122, 123, 124, 125, 126 and 127 from *The Collected Poems of Wilfred Owen* to Harold Owen and Chatto and Windus Ltd; for 30 to Penguin Books Ltd; for 4 to Ted Hughes; for 14 and 166 from *Aspects of Proteus* by Hyam Plutzik to Harper and Row Inc.; for 17 to Mrs Hyam Plutzik; for 62 to Faber and Faber Ltd; for 145 and 149 from *Oddments, Inklings, Omens, Moments* by Alastair Reid to Little Brown and

Company Inc., J. M. Dent and Sons Ltd and Laurence Pollinger Ltd; for 11 and 16 from *Collected Poems* by Isaac Rosenberg to Chatto and Windus Ltd; for 137 to Justin St John; for 18 from *The People, Yes*, 49 and 75 from *Smoke and Steel*, 88, 168 and 176 from *Good Morning, America* and 160 from *Slabs of the Burning West* by Carl Sandburg to Harcourt, Brace and World Inc.; for 6 and 128 from *Poems New and Selected* by Jon Silkin to Chatto and Windus Ltd; for 114 to Charles Scribner's Sons; for 15 to the Fulcrum Press; for 24 from Frances Ademola (ed.), *Reflections*, to Wole Soyinka and African Universities Press; for 33, 92, 130, 158 and 163 from *The Rescued Year* by William Stafford to Harper and Row Inc.; for 138 and 157 to William Stafford; for 109 and 142 from *Out of Bounds* and 174 from *The Astronomy of Love* by Jon Stallworthy to the Oxford University Press; for 61, 98, 131, 151 and 156 to Faber and Faber Ltd; for 74 from *Collected Poems* by Dylan Thomas to J. M. Dent and Sons Ltd and the Trustees for the Copyright of the late Dylan Thomas; for 153 to Mrs Myfanwy Thomas; for 16, 32 and 154 from *American Scenes* by Charles Tomlinson to the Oxford University Press; for the translations of 27 and 28 to New American Library Inc.; for the translations of 19 and 29 from *Antiworlds* by Andrei Voznesensky to the Oxford University Press; for 44 from *The Nesting Ground* by David Wagoner to Indiana University Press; for the translations of 66, 70 and 174 to Constable and Co. Ltd; for 31 to the Macmillan Company of New York; for 38 and 159 to Faber and Faber Ltd; for 9 from *Pictures from Brueghel and Other Poems* by William Carlos Williams to MacGibbon and Kee Ltd; for 63 and 133 from *The Collected Poems of W. B. Yeats* to M. B. Yeats and Macmillan and Co. Ltd.

Pictures   For the picture on page 6 to the Ashmolean Museum, Oxford; page 17 to Lawrence Darton; page 19 to Saul Steinberg and the World Publishing Company Inc.; pages 20–21 to Saul Steinberg and Hamish Hamilton Ltd; page 23 to the Trustees of the National Gallery; pages 27, 33 and 173 to Roger Mayne; page 29 to James Hogg; page 35 to Peter Blake and the Trustees of the Tate Gallery; page 45 to the John Hillelson Agency Ltd (Magnum Photos); page 47 to Bill Brandt; page 55 to the Fogg Art Museum, Harvard University (Gift of Meta and Paul J. Sachs); page 61 to the Rheinisches Landesmuseum, Bonn; pages 109 and 110 to the Black Star Publishing Company Ltd; page 111 to Keystone Press Agency Ltd; page 114 to the Walker Art Gallery, Liverpool; pages 119, 120, 122 and 124 to the Radio Times Hulton Picture Library; pages 121 and 123 to the Imperial War Museum; pages 134–5 to Gala Film Distributors Ltd; pages 136–7 to the Musées Royaux des Beaux Arts, Brussels; page 148 to the Trustees of the Tate Gallery; page 152 to the Trustees of the British Museum.

Every effort has been made to trace owners of copyright material, but in some cases this has not proved possible. The publishers would be glad to hear from any further copyright owners of material reproduced in *Voices*.

List of Illustrations

page 6   *Self Portrait*, painting by Samuel Palmer

17   *The Towel Merchant Takes a Much Needed Rest*, photograph by A. W. Cutler, taken in New York in 1908

19   *The Subway*, drawing by Saul Steinberg

20–1   *Line Drawing*, drawing by Saul Steinberg

23   *Cart*, detail from *The Château of Steen*, painting by Sir Peter Paul Rubens

27   *Wole Soyinka*, photograph by Roger Mayne

29   *Motorway Bridge*, photograph by James Hogg

33   *Actors with Masks*, photograph by Roger Mayne

35   *On the Balcony*, painting by Peter Blake

45   *Burning of the Passes*, photograph by Ian Berry

47   *Coal Searchers in Jarrow*, photograph by Bill Brandt

55   *Blind Botanist*, drawing by Ben Shahn

61   *The Roettgen Pietà*, anonymous woodcarving, German, about 1300

81   *The Chain Shop*, anonymous photograph taken in 1910

103   *The Deathbed*, woodcut by Edvard Munch

109   *Dead Mother and Child at Don Xoai*, anonymous photograph

110   *American Soldier and Vietnamese Mother*, anonymous photograph

111   *Individual Air Raid Shelters in Hanoi*, anonymous photograph

  Friendship Through Music, anonymous photograph

114   *Fallen Warrior*, sculpture by Henry Moore

119   *Recruiting Office at Southwark Town Hall*, anonymous photograph

  French Boys of 18 Join Up, anonymous photograph

  King's Royal Rifle Corps Recruiting March, anonymous photograph

120   *American Troops at Entrance to Shell-Proof Dugout*, anonymous photograph

121   *Difficulties Encountered in Bringing Supplies to the Front*, anonymous photograph

122   *French Troops Make a Raid on a German Trench*, anonymous photograph

123   *The Germans Fail to Bury Their Dead*, anonymous photograph

124   *Ruined Street in Ypres*, anonymous photograph

134–5   *The Dance of Death*, still photograph from *The Seventh Seal*, a film by Ingmar Bergman

136–7   *The Fall of Icarus*, painting by Pieter Brueghel the Elder

145   *Wrestlers*, woodcut by Hokusai

148   *Bird*, sculpture by Elizabeth Frink

152   *The Cock Fight*, engraving by William Hogarth

173   *Girl on a Bus*, photograph by Roger Mayne

176   *Endpiece*, woodcut by Hokusai

Index of Titles

Numbers refer to the numbers of poems

A Boy's Head, 167
A Day with the Foreign Legion, 31
A January Night, 164
A Living, 36
A Sane Revolution, 52
A Survey, 138
A Thousand Years, 79
Africa's Plea, 22
After Long Drought, 137
After Looking into a Book Belonging
   to my Great-Grandfather Eli Eliakim
   Plutzik, 17
All-In Wrestlers, 144
An Empty Threat, 162
Anecdote from Talk, 40
Angry Samson, 39
Anthem for Doomed Youth, 119
As Kingfishers Catch Fire, 23
As Others See Us, 20
As Sure as What is Most Sure, 173
At a Calvary Near the Ancre, 126
At Day-Close in November, 165

Ballad, 76
Ballad of the Bread Man, 55
Ballade, 27
Beautiful Old Age, 45
Before Life and After, 118
Birds, 146
Black Rook in Rainy Weather, 4
Blue Umbrellas, 152
Brothers, 59
Bullocky, 42

Cat-Faith, 145
Cat-Goddesses, 81
Chief Standing Water, 32
Courage, 47
Days, 3
Death, 132
Death and the Maiden, 102
Defence, 128
Desert Places, 139
Domination of Black, 131
Don't Sign Anything, 57

Effort at Speech Between Two People,
   97
Elegy for Alfred Hubbard, 43
Elegy for Simon Corl, Botanist, 44
Epitaph, 106
Epitaph on a Tyrant; 50

F for Francis, 178
Father and Child, 63
Father Dunman's Funeral, 107
Felix Randal, 171
Follower, 13
Footnote to John ii, 4, 53
For Ann, 82
For Sale, 105
Four Orders, 8
Fragment XXXVII, 11
Frankie and Johnny, 89
Frogs, 7
From William Tyndale to John Frith,
   35
Futility, 123

Georgian Marketplaces, 19
Girls in a Factory, 77
Go By Brooks, 78
God's Grandeur, 148

Hay for the Horses, 15
Hazardous Occupations, 160
He Was, 38
Home Burial, 101
How to Paint a Perfect Christmas, 169
Hurt Hawks, 143

I Am, 21
Ice-Fishing, 158
I'm Older than You, Please Listen, 56
In my Craft or Sullen Art, 74
It Sifts from Leaden Sieves, 155
It's Coming, 103

Jazz Fantasia, 75
Jesus and his Mother, 54
Judgements, 33
Juggler, 159

Lament, 174
Leader of Men, 51
Love Comes Quietly, 93
Love Will Find Out The Way, 68
Lovers in Winter, 95

Memories of a Lost War, 114
Merritt Parkway, 26
Musée des Beaux Arts, 133
My Busconductor, 41
My Tangled Hair, 80

Names, 141
Nationality, 112

O Taste and See, 1
On a Painted Woman, 69
On Thomas Bond and his Wife, 91
Ou Phrontis, 90
Our City is Guarded by Automatic
    Rockets, 130

Paradise, 58
Pass Office Song, 34
Passing Remark, 92
Patterns of Earth, 166
People Hide their Love, 70
Pigeons, 149
Plucking the Rushes, 66
Public Bar TV, 140

Room for a Blade of the Town, 48

Sair Fyeld, Hinny, 46
Sayings from the Northern Ice, 157
Sea Chest, 88
She's like the Swallow, 86
Snatch of Sliphorn Jazz, 176
Snow, 153
Snow Drop, 6
Song, 83
Sonnet, 136
Sonnet on Seeing a Piece of our Artil-
    lery Brought into Action, 122
Soup, 49
Strange Meeting, 127
Strawberries, 64
Summer Farm, 25

Tea, 98
Telephone Conversation, 24
The Chinaman and the Florentine, 14
The Clock-Winder, 73
The Clod and the Pebble, 99
The Debate between Villon's Heart
    and Body, 28
The Dying Soldier, 116
The End, 125
The Enlisted Man, 129
The Garden, 62
The Garden of Love, 100
The Last Mystery, 109
The Latest Decalogue, 113
The Loving Dexterity, 9
The Magpies, 94
The Midnight Skaters, 161
The Mother's Song, 10
The Next War, 121
The Nose, 29
The Parable of the Old Men and the
    Young, 124
The People, Yes, 18
The Performance, 115
The Picnic, 65
The Plot against the Giant, 61
The Red Cockatoo, 147
The Royal Duke of Grantham, 85
The Secret, 175
The Sick Rose, 71
The Snow Fences, 154
The Snow Man, 156
The Swan, 5
The Telephone, 96
The Trap, 142
The Twin of Sleep, 135
The Unquiet Grave, 72
Then my Love and I'll be Married, 60
There's Been a Death, 104
Thirteen Ways of Looking at a Black-
    bird, 151
Thistles, 172
To an Old Lady, 12
To My Dear and Loving Husband, 87
Two Wise Generals, 117

Upon his Departure, Hence, 108
Useless, 177
Ute Mountain, 16

Vacation, 163
Voices, 120

Wanting the Impossible, 168
Water, 134
Wedgebury Cocking, 150
Well Water, 2

We'll Go No More A-roving, 84
What Is He?, 37
What Were They Like?, 111
When Molly Smiles, 67
Where Are You Now, Batman?, 30
Wings, 170
Wreaths, 110

Index of First Lines

Numbers refer to the numbers of poems

A ball will bounce, but less and less. It's not, 159
a brown old man with a green thumb, 38
A faithless shepherd courted me, 76
A man should never earn his living, 36
A perverse habit of cat-goddesses, 81
A skein of suns, the uncut stones of night, 141
A thousand years, you said, 79
A tight-lipped hermit, parched of sounds, 137
A time there was – as one may guess, 118
About suffering they were never wrong, 133
Above, you paint the sky, 169
After the blast of lightning from the East, 125
Against the rubber tongues of cows and the hoeing hands of men, 172
Among the twenty snowy mountains, 151
Are they blind, the lords of Gaza, 39
Are you happy? It's the only, 176
As a cat, caught by the door opening, 145
As if it were, 26
As kingfishers catch fire, dragonflies dráw fláme, 23
As sure as what is most sure, sure as that spring primroses, 173
At night, by the fire, 131
At Wedgebury there was a cocking, 150

Be slowly lifted up, thou long black arm, 122
Because I have no time, 174
Beside his heavy-shouldered team, 42
Bottomed by tugging combs of water, 5
Breaking every law except the one, 130
Bugles sang, saddening the evening air, 120
'Bury me on a Sunday', 107

Chief Standing Water, 32

Death is the twin of Sleep, they say, 135
Did the people of Viet Nam, 111

Don't throw your arms around me in that way, 53
Down in the Frantic Mountains, 138
Down with all Raphaels, 19
Drum on your drums, batter on your banjoes, 75

Each day the tide withdraws; chills us; pastes, 110

F for Francis, 178
Felix Randal the farrier, O is he dead then? my duty all ended, 171
Frankie and Johnny were lovers, 89
Frogs sit more solid, 7

Go by brooks, love, 78
Green rushes with red shoots, 66
Green thoughts are, 11

He had driven half the night, 15
He knew that coastline – no man better, 109
He saw her from the bottom of the stairs, 101
'Here are houses,' he moaned, 116
Here lie the bodies, 91
How lovely the elder brother's, 59
Hubbard is dead, the old plumber, 43

I accuse, 33
I am a trembling leaf, 8
I am not you, 22
I am troubled by the blank fields, the speechless graves, 17
I am – yet what I am, none cares or knows, 21
I blesse thee, Lord, because I GROW, 58
I have grown past hate and bitterness, 112
I saw a famous man eating soup, 49
I stay, 162
I went to the Garden of Love, 100
If ever two were one, then surely we, 87
If I were called in, 134
If you make a revolution, make it for fun, 52
I'll come to thee at even tide, 83
In it there is a space-ship, 167
In my craft or sullen art, 74
In scenery I like flat country, 92
In the gloom of whiteness, 153
'Isn't that an iceberg on the horizon, Captain?', 18
It is dark as a cave, 73
It is people at the edge who say, 157
It is so still in the house, 10
It is the picnic with Ruth in the spring, 65
It ought to be lovely to be old, 45
It seemed that out of battle I escaped, 127
It sifts from Leaden Sieves, 155

It's coming – the postponeless Creature, 103

John Watson was a tin-mine man, 40
Jugglers keep six bottles in the air, 160

Like a skein of loose silk blown against a wall, 62
Love comes quietly, 93
'Love seeketh not itself to please', 99

Mary stood in the kitchen, 55
Move him into the sun, 123
My busconductor tells me, 41
My father worked with a horse-plough, 13
My only son, more God's than mine, 54
My tangled hair, 80

Nor dread nor hope attend, 132
'Not as Black Douglas, bannered, trumpeted', 117
Not thinking other than how the hand works, 158
Now the new grass is vivid with dandelions, 166

O rose, thou art sick !, 71
O soft embalmer of the still midnight, 136
On a flaked ridge of the desert, 140
On one of those days with the Legion, 31
On the crooked arm of Columbus, on his cloak, 149
On the stiff twig up there, 4
Once I saw a grown man fall from a tree, 102
One ever hangs where shelled roads part, 126
One must have a mind of winter, 156
One scene as I bow to pour her coffee, 163
Out there, we've walked quite friendly up to Death, 121
Over the mountains, 68

Perfection, of a kind, was what he was after, 50
Periwinks, periwinkle, 106
Poor sheepish plaything, 105

Riding the horse as was my wont, 57
Ripeness is all ; her in her cooling planet, 12
Room, room for a Blade of the Town, 48

Sair fyeld, hinny, sair fyeld now, 46
Seated in rows at the machines, 77
Sent as a present from Annam, 147
She arrived late, with this motto, 128
She hears me strike the board and say, 63
She's like the swallow that flies so high, 86
Six dukes went a-fishing, 85

Snow falling and night falling fast, oh, fast, 139
So Abram rose, and clave the wood, and went, 124
So much the goat scratches he can't sleep, 27
So we'll go no more a-roving, 84
Speak to me. Take my hand. What are you now?, 97
Straws like tame lightnings lie about the grass, 25
Suppose he wishes balloon routes, 168

Take off your hat, 34
The after-thought, 177
The bells assault the maiden air, 90
The blanched melted snows, 6
The broken pillar of the wing jags from the clotted shoulder, 143
The first night that the monster lurched, 142
The flower, 9
The guns know what is what, but underneath, 114
The hop-poles stand in cones, 161
The last time I saw Donald Armstrong, 115
The letters I, your lone friend, write in sorrow, 35
The posture of the tree, 95
The price seemed reasonable, location, 24
The rain smites more and more, 164
The ten hours' light is abating, 165
'The thing that makes a blue umbrella with its tail', 152
'The wind doth blow today, my love', 72
The world is, 1
The world is charged with the grandeur of God, 148
There was a woman loved a man, 88
There were never strawberries, 64
There's been a Death, in the Opposite House, 104
These two great men battling like lovers, 144
They are fencing the upland against, 154
This man for forty years studied a leaf, 14
Thou shalt have one God only; who, 113
Thus I, 108
To the young man I would say, 56
To youths, who hurry thus away, 69
Two girls discover, 175

We have, 170
What a girl called 'the dailiness of life', 2
What are days for?, 3
What is he?, 37
What makes people unsatisfied, 47
What passing-bells for these who die as cattle, 119
Whatever the bird is, is perfect in the bird, 146
When he addressed ten thousand, 51
'When I am gone', 16
'When I was just as far as I could walk', 96

When Molly smiles beneath her cow, 67
When roses grow on thistle tops, 60
When the elephant's-ear in the park, 98
When this yokel comes maundering, 61
When Tom and Elizabeth took the farm, 94
Where are you now, Batman? Now that Aunt Heriot has reported Robin
    missing, 30
Who says that it's by my desire, 70
Who's that I hear? *It's me*. Who? *Your heart*, 28
With Annie gone, 82
With 'No Admittance' printed on my heart, 20
With wild flowers bedded in his mind, 44

Yelled Corporal Punishment at Private Reasons, 129
Yesterday my doctor told me, 29

Index of Poets, Translators and Collectors

Numbers refer to the numbers of poems

W. H. Auden, 29, 50, 132

William Blake, 71, 99, 100
Edmund Blunden, 161
Ronald Bottrall, 8
Edgar Bowers, 35
Geoffrey Bownas, 79, 80
Anne Bradstreet, 87
Georges de Brébeuf, 69
Lord Byron, 84

Charles Causley, 55, 90
John Clare, 21, 76, 83
Arthur Hugh Clough, 113
Leonard Cohen, 78, 82
Tony Connor, 43
Robert Creeley, 57, 93

Roland Tombekai Dempster, 22
James Dickey, 115
Emily Dickinson, 103, 104, 155
Basil Dowling, 20

William Empson, 12, 40
D. J. Enright, 152

A. R. D. Fairburn, 56
Peter Freuchen, 10
Robert Frost, 96, 101, 139, 162
Roy Fuller, 141

Mary Gilmore, 112
Denis Glover, 77, 94
Robert Graves, 39, 81, 95, 129, 135
Thom Gunn, 54

Thomas Hardy, 73, 107, 118, 164, 165
Max Hayward, 19
Seamus Heaney, 13
Lady Heguri, 79
George Herbert, 58
Robert Herrick, 108
Geoffrey Hill, 110
Miroslav Holub, 167, 169, 170
Gerard Manley Hopkins, 23, 59, 148,
    171, 173
Ted Hughes, 117, 140, 172

Randall Jarrell, 2
Robinson Jeffers, 143

John Keats, 136
James Kirkup, 144
Galway Kinnell, 27, 28

Philip Larkin, 3, 134
D. H. Lawrence, 36, 37, 45, 47, 52
Denise Levertov, 1, 26, 111, 175
John Logan, 65
Robert Lowell, 105

Norman MacCaig, 7, 25, 51
R. A. K. Mason, 53
Roger McGough, 41
Ian Milner, 167, 169
Edwin Morgan, 64

Howard Nemerov, 102
G. F. Northall, 177, 178

Wilfred Owen, 119–27

Brian Patten, 30
Sylvia Plath, 4
Hyam Plutzik, 14, 17, 166
Ezra Pound, 62

Alastair Reid, 145, 149
John Wilmot, Second Earl of
    Rochester, 48
W. R. Rodgers, 5
Isaac Rosenberg, 11, 16
Muriel Rukeyser, 97

Peggy Rutherfoord, 34

Justin St John, 137
Carl Sandburg, 18, 49, 75, 88, 160,
    168, 176
Percy Bysshe Shelley, 69
Jon Silkin, 6, 128
Louis Simpson, 114
Gary Snyder, 15
Wole Soyinka, 24
William Stafford, 33, 92, 130, 138,
    157, 158, 163
Jon Stallworthy, 109, 142, 174
Wallace Stevens, 61, 98, 131, 151, 156

George Theiner, 169, 170
Dylan Thomas, 74
Edward Thomas, 153
Anthony Thwaite, 79, 80
Charles Tomlinson, 16, 32, 154

Francois Villon, 27, 28
Andrei Voznesensky, 19, 29

David Wagoner, 44
Arthur Waley, 66, 70, 147
Reed Whittemore, 31
Richard Wilbur, 38, 159
William Carlos Williams, 9
Judith Wright, 42, 146
Wu-Ti, 70

W. B. Yeats, 63, 133